D1604469

The Faithful Witness

The Faithful Witness

A Pastmillenial Study of Revelation

Ken Gore

VANTAGE PRESS
New York

All Biblical scripture quoted herein is from the *New American Standard Bible*, Copyright © The Lockman Foundation 1960, 1962, 1963, 1968, 1971, 1972, 1973, 1975, 1977. Used by permission.

Contents

Foreword

What is the Book of Revelation all about? How you answer that question will determine how you interpret the Book of Revelation. Is it all about the past, the future? Whose future? Is it about Good vs. Evil in a timeless way which could fit any situation? or is it a History of the Church? or is it a Drama of the Glory of God?

Reading the Book of Revelation without the help of a thought-out context will lead to more questions than answers. Chapter 1 has some symbolic language, but it is understandable all the way through chapter 4. When we get to Chapter 20:11 and following to the end of the book we recognize the last judgment, Heaven, Hell. The problem we face is in Chapters 5–20:10. The symbolic language used can be forced into different contexts. What is the context? What does it mean?

The answer to that question will not only determine how you read Revelation, but it will also determine how you read the rest of the prophecy of the Bible, how you look at current events, what churches you can be a member of, and which schools you can attend. You will be shunned and even hated by some misled brothers and sisters in Christ for differing on this point.

If you begin a study of Revelation already believing what it is about, you will interpret the Book to go where you thought it would. There must be a point in time when each of us objectively looks at all the different views of good Bible-believing Christian scholars, to determine which one best fits the Book itself. I have gone through this process and have come to a position that is different from the one I used to have. It is a position on the Millennium that I have not been able to find in other books (although I believe it is out there somewhere).

Therefore, I have written this book, which is about a different Millennial view. To put that view in its context I felt it important to comment on Revelation, because I have come to believe that the book is not about our future, but about witnessing. I believe the basic message of the book is too many times lost in the details of the book. In further study I have come to believe that the Millennium is also (compared to the book as a whole) a detail, in that it only appears in a few verses and does not give us a lot of explanation of what it is.

This work will proceed with an introduction which is important in any study of Revelation, because the style of writing an apocalypse is so different from other scripture. The introduction will be followed by a verse-by-verse commentary on the Book of Revelation stressing what I believe the book stresses. Because I have come to believe that the Millennium is not a major factor in the Book of Revelation, my view is merely stated in the commentary, and after the commentary I will explain and defend this new view. I am grateful to all the wise men whose words I have read in studying this great book. If I have helped you to understand more of God's word I credit the Holy Spirit and the great men whose shoulders I have stood on; most of their names are to be found in the bibliography. Others include Dr. George Jennings and other teachers at California Baptist University (at that time College); Dr. Fred Fisher, and other fine teachers at Gold Gate Baptist Theological Seminary. Appreciation also goes to godly pastors under whom I have had the privilege to sit, among others who have shaped my thinking.

If I confuse you, that is my own personality coming out in the writing. If you don't like my different approach, do not blame these Godly men who are not guilty of my misunderstandings. I take none of the credit, all of the blame, and whatever else the IRS leaves me.

I also want to thank Elizabeth for editings and making helpful suggestions and the fine work done by the good folk at Vantage Press.

Introduction

I. Presuppositions

Because this is my book and there are some things that I am going to assume, you need to know what those things are. These assumptions will be a starting point for discussion and will not be argued here.

The Bible Is the Word of God

This seems simple for anyone writing about the Bible, but unfortunately it is not always the case. Sometimes those who write about the Bible do so from an academic view but not always from a view of faith. Even more unfortunately some of those who profess the faith have bought into theories that deny that God wrote the Bible. I am a pastor and not an academician, and I hope to write this book well enough so as not to embarrass my teachers, but simply enough to communicate to all. The Book of Revelation was written for all, and so books about it should be written for all.

Exactly how God wrote the Bible is beyond our scope of discussion in this book. Just note that I believe all 66 books are the word of God, and have authority; that is, they must be obeyed. (For those who are interested, I believe Article One of the Baptist Faith and Message, and agree with the Chicago Statement on Biblical Hermeneutics.)

The Gospel

The Faith mentioned above is the Christian Faith and not any other. (Yes, it does make a difference.) It is (but is not limited to) the belief that God became man in the person of Jesus Christ, lived a perfect life, died on a cross for our sins, and rose on the third day. Because He died for our sins, we who believe can be free from the guilt and power of sin. Believers gather themselves into fellowships called churches and wait for the second coming of Jesus, which could be at any moment. He will come in power and for judgment.

At this point you may be saying, "how nice for you;" yet just as it is unbelievable that there are those who will write about the book and not believe, there are also those who have read about the Book of Revelation and don't believe. Let me say a word to you. The Book of Revelation is a book from God to a believer for other believers. If you continue to remain on the outside not only will this book always be a mystery to you, but so will life.

God loved you so much that He sent His son to die for your sins, so that if you will believe in Him you will have everlasting life. Everlasting life is a higher quality of life which includes a personal relationship with Jesus. He does not hate you, He loves you enough to die for you. He has the best plan for your life (He is smarter than you are). You need to submit your life to Him. He is Lord!

"How do I do this?" you may ask. Pray, right now; confess that you are a sinner (Romans 3:23 "for all have sinned and fall short of the glory of God"), and repent of your sins (He will forgive you and help you turn from your sins). Believe in Jesus. Thank Him for dying for your sins, and rising again from the dead. (Romans 10:9 and 10 . . . "if you confess with your mouth Jesus as Lord, and believe in your heart that God raised Him from the dead, you shall be saved; for with the heart man believes, resulting in righteousness, with the mouth he confesses, resulting in salvation'').

If I have not explained this clearly enough, God has placed in your life a Christian who can explain it to you better. Find that person and ask him or her for guidance. Do it now.

If you will do this you will begin a new life. 2 Corinthians 5:17 "Therefore if any man is in Christ, he is a new creature; the old things passed away; behold, new things have come.'' If you don't, this same Jesus who could have saved you will be your Judge while your sins still cling to you. This we will see in the Book of Revelation. There are only two kinds of people on the earth: believers and non-believers. Which will you be?

Now you may be asking, "If I did this, what do I do now?'' Tell a Christian friend. Find a Bible-believing, Christ-honoring Church where the Bible is taught. As the Spirit leads you, join it, support it, obey what Christ tells you through it. It takes a moment to become a Christian, it takes a lifetime to learn to live holy. Read the Bible and pray daily; this is life for you.

Who, When, and Where

Who wrote the Book of Revelation? God wrote the Bible, by revealing Himself to men. How this is done is a subject of much discussion, but not for this book. In the Book of Revelation we are not left to speculate, according to Chapter 1 verse 1. God gave this Revelation to Jesus who gave it to John through his Angel.

Now the question is, "which John?'' I believe it is the same Apostle John who was the brother of James, son of

Zebedee. For more information on John, see the section "I, John," in Chapter 1. For a discussion on the identity of the author of Revelation, see the Introduction to Summers, or Swete, or others who care to chase this rabbit.

When was it written? I believe it was A.D. 90. You will find some who will put it in the '60s during Nero's time. This would not make much difference, but I will go with the majority opinion here.

Where was it written? It was written on the prison island of Patmos. John was under arrest for preaching the Word. He wrote to seven churches just across the water on what is now the west coast of Turkey. The main focus of the book is these seven churches in Asia Minor and that time period.

The objection might be raised, "Well, if it was for that time why should I read it now?" No one ever raises this objection to I Corinthians or Galatians. While I & II Corinthians, Galatians, and indeed most of the New Testament letters, were to someone or some particular church with a particular problem, they are all for us to learn from. More about this in Chapters 1 & 2.

Begin at the Beginning

To begin anything we usually need to begin at the beginning. This does not mean Chapter 1 Verse 1 of Revelation. God placed this book at the end of the Scriptures for a reason. If you don't understand what is in Genesis, Exodus, Isaiah, Matthew, Mark, Acts, or Romans, what are you doing here?!! John is going to refer to the whole Bible in this letter and a working knowledge of those books needs to come first. This is really true if you are a new Christian. If you are a new Christian, begin with the Gospel of Mark or John, Genesis, or I & II Samuel. Eat freely of the meat before you chew on the bone. This is why Revelation is not at the beginning, it is the end.

A toddler at home with his mom would hear "No!" as he began to put his fingers in a light socket. She may spank his hand to keep him from harm. She may also have the same reaction to a Republican. The child will learn to avoid light sockets and Republicans. Later as the child grows he will see that there is a difference between the danger electricity has for a small child, and the political views of his mother. The mother is not wrong to warn her child of danger, even if he eventually becomes a Republican electrician. At a young age one is not able to handle difficult and dangerous things, and should not. With growth, maturity, and a skill at handling the Word of God we are better equipped to handle things than we were before.

A pastor or evangelist may rightly warn his people about heretics, theological liberals who do not believe the Bible, and those people who would lead them to sin and to Hell. With the same voice and tone he may push his own view of Revelation, and attack as "Liberal" anyone who disagrees. As with the mother, the pastor or evangelist must warn his people about the real dangers to their soul, and he should not insert his opinion as fact. However, like the mother, he may not do all that much damage. People grow and mature and no longer see the world in categories of white and black, good and bad, any more. People move from "is this person good or bad," to "is this idea true or false." A bad person can say a true thing and a good person say a false thing. People grow spiritually and mentally and begin to ask, not "is he safe?" but "is it true?"

What is the standard if we cannot go by who is good and who is bad? Well—the Bible, of course. The question is does the Bible confirm or deny the words stated. It is not wrong for a young Christian, someone just converted, to look for "safe" teachers because they don't know the difference; but growth demands that we change and learn for ourselves what the Bible says. For some of you this book may be too early in your spiritual growth, and you need to read the other parts of the Bible first.

Some folks like to read the back of the book first to find out who did it. However, when you do that you do not understand the end because you missed the things that happened in between.

In Revelation the Scriptures are referred to, but not in the same way as Matthew or Paul would do. In Revelation there is no prof-text (a quote from an Old Testament source to prove a point) reference, but rather a passing reference that you need to be familiar with. Usually it does not mean that this is a fulfillment of the previous reference, just a reference to shake the memory. I will try to bring these up as I see them.

II. He Who Has an Ear . . .

This was a favorite phrase of Jesus when He was speaking to the Pharisees who loved to talk and hated to listen. When you think you know everything you tend to stop listening. Only God knows everything. God was in Christ speaking to Pharisees and religious leaders, the best of Judaism, and they would not hear him. They had everything figured out and did not need anyone to tell them what was what, not even the Messiah.

Today we are so smug in our ideas that we will not hear. We will not hear each other and sometimes we will not hear God. Jesus asks His people, in the Book of Revelation, to hear what the Spirit says to the Churches.

A Lack of Agreement in Eschatology

Welcome to the wonderful world of eschatology. "What is that?" you ask. It is the study of the Eschaton. Aren't you glad you asked? Again, "what is that?" you say. The Eschaton is a Greek term for "last," therefore eschatology is the study of the doctrine of last things. "Oh, help!" you say. Exactly. If you are not apprehensive about the study of last things you are either very secure in your salvation, or certain that your views cannot be wrong. It's the second group that I worry about.

There is a time for us to stand dogmatically on issues and doctrines. There are some truths worth dying for, there are other truths that are not even worth arguing about. The time to stand for a doctrine is when it is clearly taught in the Bible. The Trinity, the Deity of Christ, His crucifixion, His resurrection, our salvation by grace alone through faith alone. These things the Bible clearly teaches. There are times when the old saying "Good men disagree" applies. Not about the issues just raised, but about Church government, how and when to practice the Lord's Supper and Baptism, what translation of the Bible to use . . .

We all hold different beliefs on these issues and will still share the same Heaven with the same Lord. Then we will find out whether I was right, or not. These things must be taught for practical reasons but we should not fight over them. Of these we should learn from Chapter 14 of Romans, especially v. 5.

The interpretation of Revelation belongs to the set of truths where good men disagree. The churches have never been in total agreement as to what these words in Revelation mean, especially Chapters 5–19. We should not turn on our brother who disagrees with us on Revelation. There are doctrines of eschatology, which we must believe. (*see* IV. What

We Must Believe, below) The question becomes more important, "What does the Bible really say?"

Two Ways of Interpretation

There are two ways to approach the study of a difficult part of Scripture. One is, with (of course) the aid of the Holy Spirit, to use the skills of interpretation and listen to what the text says. Hear the Word of the Lord. (Having ears to hear). Collect all the evidence. Gather the thinking of others who have studied this and try to understand their thoughts. (After 2,000 years you are not the first honest student to open this book). If they are all agreed, there is no problem. If there is disagreement, keep an open mind; it's the kind of mind the Holy Spirit can really use. Follow the Spirit's leading to the most logical, wise, and practical solution that agrees with the rest of Scripture. After coming to your conclusion, because it is a disputed passage, still keep an open mind, and a kind heart and Christian disposition to those who disagree and also have the Holy Spirit.

The other way is to find out what your group believes, or what the majority of people believe, or what your favorite teacher believes, and then use the Bible to defend these important truths, no matter what. Following this method you will never be wrong in your own eyes. This is not having ears to hear with but to find fault with. There is nothing wrong with finding out what your particular church stands for and defending it. We need to do that. But we must never do that if it disagrees with Scripture. We must let the Holy Spirit use His Word to point us to the truth. The late Dr. Fred Fisher used to tell us in class that "When the Bible always agrees with you be suspicious; you're probably reading it wrong." Always check your pre-conceived notions and biases and let the Word of God speak to you in a fresh new way. Don't cut off the Holy Spirit by saying, "Yeah, I know what you mean," when you probably don't.

Importance

How important is it to get your view of Revelation perfect? Well at this point in the introduction I am supposed to say it is the most important thing in your life. However, that is not the case. Your relationship to God is the most important. There are believers who live and move and love the Lord, and do not understand the Book of Revelation any more than they understand automatic transmissions or VCRs. There are believers who go along with a popular view, or a view that their church holds, because that is what is taught; but they could come closer to understanding the national debt, or their own taxes, before they could Revelation. There are pastors who have nagging doubts and questions when they hear a zealous prophecy teacher who questions the faith of anyone who disagrees with them. I know because I was one.

Martin Luther took on the Catholic Church and began the Great Reformation. He taught Bible at Wittenburg, pastored the church in Wittenburg, translated the Bible into German. To Luther, the book of Revelation was a book of straw. John Calvin, from Switzerland, taught the world reformed theology. His teachings, books, sermons, and commentaries are still studied, yet he could not make heads nor tails of Revelation. The reformers liked the idea of Rome being the Beast, but other than that they made no dogmatic statement on what it all means; yet, they could define Christianity, correct error, and live Christian lives and set standards that still stand today. If you are not sure what

Revelation means you are not alone; as a matter of fact you are in very good company. Perhaps the reformers understood that salvation is by Grace and not by what you believe about the four horses.

All the major doctrines of the Bible are found outside of the Book of Revelation. Even if you never understand the Book of Revelation you can love the Lord, serve His Church, witness for Him, and grow in Grace.

If this is true, why try? Why not just ignore it? Because I believe that on this point Luther was wrong. The Book of Revelation is the Word of God. I think it has an important message for our age. Others think it has a different message; for some the interpretation of Revelation is just there to tell us about our future. If this is true it will tell you about what God will do; there is nothing we can do about it, and until it happens it does not relate to our lives.

Any study of a New Testament book includes great interest in who the first readers were and what they were going through at the time it was written. Unfortunately that is not the approach usually followed for Revelation, and therefore a different message is obtained. I believe the original message is just as important today as it was then, because the world is not much different. Revelation is not the ravings of an old madman, it is the vital message of Jesus to churches in trouble. I urge you to make an attempt to learn the message of this book; it will be worth it.

III. What We Must Believe

We must believe the Bible teaches. There are things that the Bible clearly states about end times. There are things all believers understand about the end times. Jesus is coming back (Acts 1:11). The dead in Christ will rise first (I Corinthians 15). Jesus will judge the world (Matthew 25). There will be a New Heaven and a New Earth (Isaiah 65:17ff). The Baptist Faith and Message of 1964 states it this way:

> God in His own time and in His own way, will bring the world to its appropriate end. According to His promise, Jesus Christ will return personally and visibly in glory to the earth; the dead will be raised; and Christ will judge all men in righteousness. The unrighteous will be consigned to Hell, the place of everlasting punishment. The righteous in their resurrected and glorified bodies will receive their reward and will dwell forever in Heaven with the Lord.

This is what the Bible plainly teaches and this is what all Bible believers teach. Now some who believe the Bible believe there is more to what the Bible teaches, but I am now talking about what is essential. No matter what disagreements come later, this is what all Christians believe that the Bible says.

IV. What We Cannot Know (But Like to Guess At)

There is one more essential in eschatology, which is often forgotten and needs to be brought up from time to time. No one knows when Jesus will return except God Himself. It is a secret known only to Him. Jesus told us this in Matthew 24:36. The Greek word from which we get "mystery" is not the same idea of mystery we have today, as in the murder mysteries in which (if the authors are fair, GOOD LUCK) and if you are very clever, you will be able to figure it out. The Biblical idea of mystery is that God knows it and you don't and you will not know it until He reveals it to you. If I say that I am thinking of a number from one to a hundred you will never know for sure which number it is until I tell you. It's that kind of a mystery. Even a team of scientists cannot by taking the numbers from the Bible, figure out when Christ will return. It cannot be done!!!

Furthermore, it is none of your business. What do I mean? Well, after the Resurrection of our Lord, His disciples gathered around and said, Lord this is great that you bought our salvation, we understand that part but, " . . . is it at this time You are restoring the kingdom of Israel?" (Acts 1:6–8) "He said to them, 'It is not for you to know times or epochs which the Father has fixed by His own authority; but you shall be My witnesses both in Jerusalem, and in all Judea and Samaria, and even to the remotest part of the earth.' " We preach a lot on verse 8, but we need to go back to verse 7. "It is not for you to know" means it is none of your business. If you understand what "none of your business" means you can skip to page xxiii. Do you think Jesus would not tell the apostles and disciples he spent three years with, and then he would tell you or someone around today?! Read Matthew 24 and 25 again.

The whole point of no man knowing is so that you would always be ready. Therefore God has no desire to tell anyone. You have a better chance of finding out who "Deep Throat" was. You have a better chance of finding out what happened to Amelia Earhart. You have a better chance of finding Jimmy Hoffa's body.

A study of Revelation will never, never, never, never, never (can I use enough nevers?) give you a clue as to when Jesus is coming back. **It is the historic teaching of the Christian Church that Jesus is coming soon.** We have been here in the "last days" 2,000 years according to 1 John 2:18; and we may be here another 2,000 years or even more. Or Jesus could come at this very hour, minute, second. He will come when the Father says come, and that will be soon. By soon, I mean that we won't be ready. Every child takes a little more that 20 years to grow up, for them it is a lifetime. For the parents it's too soon.

This warning will not prevent some fool or conman inside or outside of the Church from declaring a date for the return of Christ and the end of the world. Hopefully it will stop some of you from following them. When someone sets a date by "careful study of the Word" or by "special revelation," run, do not walk, to the nearest exit. That person is a fool or a conman, but defiantly he has made a false prophecy, and anyone who gives him money joins in his folly. Christians should already live as if every day is the last. So even if someone did know when Jesus was coming back, how would that change the lives of real believers?

I was at a funeral, and the funeral director, who claimed to be a deacon, told me he had a little book that gave 84 reasons why Jesus was going to return September 24, 1984. It was early in September of that year, so I said that sounds interesting send it to me on the 25th and I will be glad to take a look at it.

"Oh," he said, "It might be the 24th or the 25th."

"Then send it on the 26th," I said.

"No, this is real. He's a rocket scientist who's become a Christian and has figured it out mathematically."

"No man knows the day or the hour . . . "

"He's got an answer for that . . . "

"There is no answer for that, but send it to me on the 27th, or the 28th, I'll take a look at it."

Well—Jesus did not return, the deacon did not send me the book (although I have many other books by others making the same claim with as much accuracy), and I understand the author came up with 85 reasons for the next year, but ever fewer people cared. This is another thing we can know for sure, Jesus is coming soon to judge the earth and no one knows when that will be, so we should always be ready.

The point of eschatology in the New Testament is to get us to live better lives, not to act goofy and make false claims.

Be Flexible

I believe that when the Book of Revelation was delivered to the seven churches, they understood it. I believe that other churches in the same circumstances also understood its clear teachings. But over time, different teachers—for different reasons—saw different things in the symbolism of Revelation. Today good men disagree. In the study of eschatology good, honest, hard-working, intelligent, Christian, Bible-believing, Bible-loving scholars disagree.

It does not help anyone to call names or to question the spirituality of, or break fellowship with, brothers who see it differently. We have talked about the things that must be believed, but there are and have been historically, disagreements that until the Lord comes back we have no way to resolve.

When good men agree, you are on solid ground. You have a solid doctrine of the Christian Church! Proclaim it, believe it, teach it, live it, and be prepared to die for it. When good men disagree, find out *why* they disagree. Question everyone and listen to the answers. Follow the reasoning and see if it holds up, or how it compares to the other fellow's. Read all sides of the argument. Stick close to the text and the context. Be open to the Holy Spirit's leading and be prepared to disagree agreeably. Be firm in your beliefs but be open to the possibility that you are wrong. You are not the only one who has the Holy Spirit.

Most of all be Christian. It is not wrong to fill in the gaps when the facts are scarce, and come up with a theory that makes sense of the Scripture. It is wrong and unChristian to attack the motives or salvation of those who come up with another theory. I am not talking about essentials; I am talking about where good men disagree.

It is okay to go out on a limb to make sense of Scripture, but remember, we are not on solid ground but in a tree house. Don't put the piano over here. When you are on solid ground you can stand firm and make weighty pronouncements. When you are out on a limb be gentle, and walk softly.

Therefore we must look at the different views that the church has come to and understand the basic differences.

V. Understanding the Major Views

Understanding the major views becomes a matter of time. In other words, for what time period was the book written? Was it written for us in the twenty-first century or for those John knew in the seven churches in the first century, or for both? Does the content describe our time or theirs, or both—or neither?

To understand Revelation it is good to read as many different views as you can get. Compare each view with the text itself and ask "does this explain the text?" You can learn something new about the book from any honest study. What you should not do is compare competing views in a verse-by-verse way. This will confuse all but the A students. The reason is that each view is going in a different direction: some into the past, some into the future. Let each author take you where he will and when you are done with that study read the Book of Revelation by itself again. I think that is a less confusing way of getting the good out of the different authors and views.

1. Past

The Preterist believes that the kingdom of God is a present as well as a future reality. The events in Revelation 4–19 depict actual events or prophecies that happened in the days in which John wrote. This view fits the Scriptures to the events of the original readers. It is rejected by many because Jesus did not return in the first century. The Preterist view is divided into two camps.

a. Radical Preterists believe that all prophecy was fulfilled in A.D. 70. Jesus returned in Judgment when the Romans destroyed the Temple (See R.C. Sproul's excellent book, *The Last Days According to Jesus*). They also believe that the Book of Revelation was written in the days of Nero and not Domitian before A.D. 70.

b. Moderate Preterist view sees most of the prophecies fitting into the first century, and other more cosmic prophecies, such as the second coming, yet to be fulfilled. The Moderate Preterist view will be the view of this book.

2. Historical

The historical view interrupts the events in Church history from Pentecost to the second coming, as revealed in chapters 4–19. Once very popular among Protestants, this view had to continue to be updated as the second coming just refused to come on time, and new history had to be refitted to the text.

3. Future

The Futurist teaches that chapters 4 through the end of the book are all about our future, or the future of our children's children. The implication is that the end is just around the corner, but because no one knows when that will be, the best way to talk about the future is to begin at the end and count backwards. "We don't know when, but when it happens it's going to be like this." The events need a recreated Roman Empire or something like it, and Irsael with a functioning Temple. Futurists are divided into 3 groups and the third is further divided into 3 groups. The first division is based on an interpretation of the two verses in the 19th chapter that describe the thousand-year reign of Christ called the "Millennium," from the Latin word for 1,000. (Much of this will be restated in the chapter called "A History of Millennial Thought.")

a. Amillennialists are not sure what those few verses in Revelation 19 mean. It's not, as their name implies, that they believe in *no* Millennium, but rather is the Millennium a symbol for something else? Does it stand for the church age? or does it mean something else? While some Futurists are Amillennialists not all Amillennialists are Futurists. The Amillennial interpretation can logically help the Preterist, and historical as well as spiritual interpretations, and while they are not all Futurists; they are lumped into this subset by those who only classify views by the one question: "What will you do with the 1,000 years?"

b. Postmillennilists believe that through the preaching of the Gospel and the effect that Christians have in the world, and through medicine, science, education, and good works, the Kingdom of God will come. Christ will reign through the church and then Jesus will come after (Post) the Millennium. This view was very popular in the last years of the nineteenth century and the early years of this century.

World War II killed this idea for most believers, and there are only a few who believe we can start again. While World War I was the "war to end all wars" and would lead to the reign of Christ and a time of peace, World War II smashed the image as one "Christian nation;" Germany brought us the Holocaust, and another "Christian nation,' the United States, brought us the atomic bomb. The Second World War brought man's regress rather than progress to the forefront. Man is still totally depraved and is not progressing to a Millennium yet.

On the other hand, those who believed this sent more missionaries, built more colleges and universities, hospitals and orphanages. If what we believe leads to what we do, then for that reason alone we should all be Postmillennialist. Those who believe the world would get worse before the end sat on their hands while the world did just that—it got worse. Maybe we should decide the meaning of the Millennium on the basis of what the Scriptures say, but do the works of Postmillennialists. While their eschatology was faulty, they believed they could change the world for the better, and they did. Those who feel smug because the future did not turn out right, need to look at the present and see how we could do better.

c. Pre-Millennialists believe that Jesus will come back before the Millennium to gather the Church together (this gathering is called the Rapture). This group is divided into 3 more groups.

1. Pre-Millennialist, Pre-trib. Most popular view among Christians in America today, this view teaches that Jesus comes back to rapture the Church before the Tribulation (Chatper 4:1) and take all believers back to Heaven while

earth begins a seven-year Tribulation described in Chapters 5–19. On Earth the Beast (or Antichrist) will take over the world (or at least the new Roman Empire), and will be the major world power. The Church is gone but 144,000 Jews convert to Christianity and begin to witness for Jesus despite heavy persecution. The Tribulation ends at the end of the seven years with the Battle of Armageddon, where the Antichrist leads the world (or at least a large coalition of nations) against Israel.

Jesus returns a second time with His saints, defeats the Antichrist, and begins the Millennium. After the Millennium ends, God will make a new Heaven and a new earth. Sometimes this view is combined with Dispensational Theology. Sometimes it has a historical view of Rev. 2 & 3, giving each Church a church age to represent the whole history of the Church, in the same way the historical view does with chapters 4–19.

2. Pre-Millennialist, Mid-trib. This view is the same as above except they place the rapture of the Church in the middle of the Tribulation (Rev. 14:14). This would mean the church would have to go through half of the Tribulation.
3. Pre-Millennialist, Post-trib. This view is the same as above except the church will go through the whole period of Tribulation before Christ comes to rapture his Church and set up the Millennium.

4. Spiritual

The Spiritual View teaches that Revelation is a symbolic book about the battle between Good and Evil, and could be applied to the past, present, and/or the future. God will win over evil and you can see this in the early churches as well as the Future.

These are the major views, and not the only views. Each has its variations, and some like to mix and match. There are good, born-again, evangelical, Bible-believing brothers and sisters in all these camps. I have heard of two other views which are really one. The Pan-millennialist, who teaches that it will all pan out in the end; and the Pro-millennialist. He's not sure what God's going to do but he is for it. You may say, "now you are being silly!" I have heard pastors speak this way and I have myself because the teachings are not conclusive. It is for this group that I am writing and hoping to give you something to cling to.

More Questions

Not only do we need to decide when these events happen, in the future or the past, we also need to decide in what order they happen. John sees this vision, and then he sees that vision. Does that mean that what he saw comes in the same order that he saw it? Are the events revealed in the order they happen or in the order that builds a better case? Could several of the visions describe the same thing even though they are not told at the same time or even near each other?

There are 3 sets of 7 : 7 Seals, 7 Trumpets, and 7 Bowls of Wrath. Each set of seven seems to end with the end of the world. Are we to understand 21 different events all happening in a row with intermissions between? Or are each 7 symbolic of the same seven events? Or does each vision speak of just a vision? Does the vision it reveals determine where it happens?

Does your head hurt yet?

VI. Learning from the First Time

When Jesus came to earth the first time, there was a lot of speculation about the Messiah: who he was, when he would come, and what he would do. There was a group that met out by the Dead Sea who thought they knew exactly what the Messiah would do. They believed that the Messiah would defeat the Romans, attack the turncoat Sadducees and the hypocritical Pharisees and come get them to establish Israel as a world power. They believed this when Jesus was born, when He taught and healed, when He died for our sins, and when He rose from the dead. At Pentecost they were still teaching what the coming Messiah would do and kept teaching it till the Roman soldiers shut them down in A.D. 70. They were at the right place at the right time and missed the Messiah because He would not follow their program. We know this because they left behind their Dead Sea Scrolls that told us all about it.

The most interesting thing to me is that Jesus did not seem to challenge the wrong eschatology of His followers or His opponents. All the Jews of Jesus' day had a world view not much different than the Dead Sea crowd. The Messiah was to bring Israel back to world leadership and get rid of the Romans. While Jesus did teach about the Kingdom of God in a different way than they were used to, at the end of the three years of teaching His disciples still believed the old idea in the upper room (John 14–16). Jesus did not waste time arguing about the end—He just declared it. It seems our eschatology in the last doctrine to change because it doesn't matter all that much, because God will do it His way, no matter what we believe. Eschatology belongs to Him.

God is in charge of the End Times and will do what He wants to do. What you or I believe about the end will not change what God has already planned to do. If we get too dogmatic about what is going to happen in the future we may not be aware of what God is doing, because it is different than what we want.

VII. Christian Life in the Nineties

What kind of world did John and the seven churches live in? What was it like to be a Christian in the first century? About half of the Church was still Jewish. Roman law stated that any religion in existence when they took over was legal but no new religion could be started. For years Christianity held legal status as a sect of Judaism. However, as more and more Gentiles who were "free from the Law" came into the Church, and after Christians escaped death in Jerusalem in A.D. 70 a break occurred between Christianity and Judaism.

Jesus prophetically predicted the end of Jerusalem and the Temple (Matt. 24), and told Christians that when the trouble comes do not run into the city, (as common defense wisdom of the day was) but to flee into the hills. As it turned out this was the best advice (of course); the carnage and tribulation inside those walls was the worst ever. Afterward, when Christians said that Jesus had told them about this, the unbelieving Jews said; 1. You made that up because you were cowards and fled Jerusalem. You manufactured this to hide the fact that you were afraid to stand for Jerusalem and the Temple. 2. You were aligned with Rome to destroy the Temple.

Judaism completed the break with Christianity by announcing in a Jewish council what is still held today: any Jew who becomes a Christian is no longer a Jew. This made Christianity a new religion and illegal under Roman law. Not that the Romans needed an excuse. Nero was the first to persecute, in an official way, Christians for being Christians. He would feed them to wild animals, put them on crosses, tie them to poles, and light them up as torches to use at his garden parties. He killed Peter and Paul in A.D. 64. This would only be the beginning of official Roman persecution.

Rome would not have to proclaim a persecution in order for local persecutions to take place. Local governments, then as now, are always looking for what we today would call federal money; they wanted to attract Rome's attention with feats of loyalty to the Emperor and by having everyone burn incense to Caesar, and say "Caesar is Lord." Pagans had no problem worshiping someone else in addition to their favorite god. Jews were exempt because their religion was legal. Christians had a real problem. Jews, upset about the Temple and the annoying way Christians had of always putting pressure on them to convert, joined with the Romans to bring persecution.

Christians had a lot of questions, such as:

1. If God loves us, why does he allow evil men to hurt us?
2. This new religion we hold is young, will it survive Roman persecution?
3. What happened to our loved ones who have died for the faith?
4. Does God even see or care about what is happening?
5. Should I burn incense to Casear?
6. If we all refuse to worship Caesar and they kill us all, how will Christianity survive?

Revelation was written to answer these questions.

VIII. What Kind of Book Is Revelation?

A. It Is an Apocalytpic Book

The word we translate "Revelation" in Greek is "Apocalypse." Apocalyptic writing was a Jewish style of underground writing. While some apocalyptic passages are found in other books of the Bible, most apocalypses are outside of Scripture. Revelation is the only complete apocalypse that is Scripture. The style goes back to the Babylonian captivity. It is both theological and political. The message of an apocalypse is basically that God is in control and will put an end to this Gentile government. Keep the faith; this too will pass away.

Apocalypses outside of the Bible are written as if they were a book of the Old Testament. It is supposed to be written by some Old Testament person and pretends to be a prophecy of the present day. Anyone familiar with the Old Testament would know: 1. This book did not belong in Scripture, but to outsiders it looked like any of their other books, and 2. It used Old Testament imagery that those of the faith would understand and those on the outside would not understand. Of necessity these books are symbolic, and are made to look to the outsider as if the book itself could be hidden among other Old Testament books. The hiding was for the protection of the reader as well as the writer. In apocalyptic writing governments and leaders are portrayed as wild and fierce animals. It is much like a written political cartoon in holy language. Apocalypses are called "tracks for hard times." The readers understood what outsiders could not.

B. It's a Symbolic Book

You will always hear someone say, "Some people take the Book of Revelation to be symbolic and we take it literally." But if you keep listening to that same person interpret the book you will hear him say, "Now this is a symbol of . . ." Everyone must at some point say that to understand the meaning of the Book. An apocalyptic book by definition is symbolic; the question is, what does the symbol mean. Symbols like the letters on this page, are symbols for words, which are symbols for ideas, which have meaning. The meaning depends on the context of when and by whom it was written. The reality is always greater than the symbol. The Lake of Fire is a symbol for the final destination of the lost, but the reality behind the symbol is greater than the symbol. To say that someone sees the book as "just symbolic," does not deal honestly with what others think. The real question is: what do the symbols mean?

One of the most prominent uses of symbols in Revelation is numbers. This is not Numerology. Do not count the words or letters and look for an interpretation. The numbers that John gives do have meaning. For this reason Roman measurements are more important than the equivalent translated into feet or miles, because the numbers would not be the same. The numbers have meaning. If you have read the Bible a lot, certain numbers become familiar. There are 12 sons of Israel, 12 tribes of Israel, 12 minor prophets, 12 apostles. Reading through the Old Testament you notice that many things happened in 40's, 12's, 7's, and 3's.

Multiples of numbers also count. When Peter asked if he should forgive his brother seven times, he probably thought he was being very generous. The answer Jesus gave was "seven times seventy." He pushed forgiveness to the limit by multiplying the question. The answer is not a number but a symbol to mean you should always forgive. There is a limit to forgiveness but if you tried to count 490 times you would lose count. The easiest way is just to forgive. One way to break down the symbol is to see what the number is made of.

3	is the number of God
$3^1/_2$	is the number of Tribulation
4	is the number of the Earth
6	is the number of sin. It is not quite 7 (missed by one sin is missing the mark.)
7	is the number of perfection 3+4
10	is the complete number 7+3
12	is the number of the people of God
24	is 12 × 2
1000	is 10 × 10 × 10
144,000	is 12 × 12 × 1,000

C. It Is a Prophetic Book

Revelation is a book of prophecy for the seven churches. Books of prophecy make up a large section of the Old Testament: from them we can understand what prophecy is. The Old Testament prophet spoke the Word of the Lord, but what was the content of that Word? One third of what the Prophets wrote was was that God had already said (usually through Moses). Another third was looking at the people of God and how they were not obeying what God had already said. We would call this application, or commentary, on the sin of the day. One third would be about the future, sometimes the near future, rarely about what we would call end times, but usually about the cross. This is according to Beecher's classic work on the Minor Prophets, *The Prophets and The Promise,* an excellent book that puts the Old Testament Prophets in perspective.

I have come to believe that the center of all prophecy is not the end times but the Cross of Jesus Christ. When you read a prophetic book in the Old Testament, and the prophet actually gets to the future, remember it's not your future, it is the prophet's future, and the Cross is in his future. The Cross is the center of God's plan. The Cross is what God wants to tell his people about. You will find some things about the end time, that is our future, but compared to the rest of prophecy, by volume it is not that much. To make up for a lack of information about the future some have come up with an idea about the double interpretation of prophecy. On occasion, a word of prophecy has two meanings, but we should not assume that is the case in every prophecy. We should assume that prophecy has only one meaning until it is proved that this particular prophecy has another meaning.

Revelation is a book of prophecy which tells the seven churches about the cross, what God has already said, what the churches need to do in the very near future, what their near future looks like and finally what will happen in the end times. The end times are not center stage of the Bible, prophecy or Revelation, the Cross is.

D. It Is an Emotional Book

John is writing from exile in a penal colony for preaching the Gospel, and writing to people who have already been under persecution and have lost loved ones to persecution.

In their near future John sees more suffering and death. As a pastor and apostle, John has a lot of emotion which reflected the emotion of Jesus who watches His people suffer. Revelation is an emotional book. Unfortunately some have absorbed the emotion and have turned it on those who take a different view of the book. You cannot read or study this book without feeling the emotion, but understand what the emotion is about. It is about the suffering of the saints.

This I believe is the context of the Book of Revelation. I therefore have placed a dedication before each chapter to those who have witnessed to the truth of the Gospel. It is good for us to know about them and it will keep us aware of the context in which Revelation is written.

E. It Is a Jewish Book Written in Greek

Revelation is written in Greek by a Christian with a Hebrew mind-set, so the language experts say. I believe that someone is the beloved disciple John. If we agree that content, purpose, and the peculiar style of an apocalypse dictates vocabulary, then the only difference in style between Revelation and John's other writings is spelling and syntax. I cannot, as some do, criticize John's Greek as it is better than mine, and I am afraid I owe much to "spell check." Evidently when John was put on the island of Patmos, the Romans did not send with him his secretary, to whom he would usually dictate. John had to write this himself. The spelling and syntax does not cause the kind of problems one would think. Everyone agrees about what John said; the question is, what does it mean?

F. It Is a Book of Praise

There is praise music all through this book. You had better get used to praising God if you want to go to Heaven, for His praises are what we sing there. While in church I prefer the older hymns, I think we need to sing good theology. I also like some of the new praise music. In Heaven we will all be able to sing better. Perhaps as you read the Book of Revelation you need to stop and sing a song of praise. It will help you get into the mood of the book. Maybe if we sang more and fought less it would also help.

IX. Majors and Minors

If you watched Disney's *Snow White*, and wondered about the significance (theological and otherwise) of the poison apple, you probably missed the point. If you have read to your child *Winnie the Pooh* and wondered if Piglet is really a Communist sympathizer, you are reading too much into things. It's a lot like the old preacher's story about the Baptist boy and the Catholic boy who decided to check out each other's churches. First the Baptist boy went with his friend to the Catholic church and the boy explained all the symbolic acts that the priest did so his friend would understand and appreciate the service. Then they went to the Baptist church, and things seem to go along quite well until just before the sermon when the pastor took off his watch and placed it on the pulpit where he could see it. The Catholic boy asked, "What does that mean?" The Baptist boy, with perfect knowledge of his church, could tell his friend, "It doesn't mean a thing."

Sometimes we miss the major things by focusing all our attention on the minor things. In the Book of Revelation it is real simple, because John makes sure to tell you what is important and what is not. When it is really important he not only repeats it, he interprets it. John himself tells you what the symbols mean. Much of the discussions on Revelation center on the minors. The four horsemen, the 144,000 and the number 666, have all caused major discussions when they are minor players in the over-all work.

The thousand-year reign of Christ is not minor to us, but it is to the over-all message of Revelation. It is only mentioned twice in the 19th chapter. We are told about what comes before and after it. The Millennium is mentioned twice but it is not interpreted, because it is not a symbol of something; rather it is, I believe, a literal 1,000 years. However, that the Millennium should dominate this book is to take things way out of proportion, because it does *not* dominate the Book of Revelation. It, like the short time that follows, is an aside to explain the time between the Tribulation that the churches were in when Revelation was written and the New Heaven and the New Earth of the future.

Well, what is "major?' If I could put the message of Revelation into one sentence it would be: "Be faithful unto death." John looks to Heaven for help for the churches he ministered to before he was put into exile on Patmos. He would have loved to aid and comfort the churches about the future.

He would have loved to tell them that this was all going to be over, and God was going to judge those responsible for persecuting the churches. What God revealed about the future is not good news. The persecution would not end. It would be necessary for believers to testify for Jesus by not burning incense to Caesar, even if it meant their death.

These are hard words. Words that John would rather not have to deliver, but it is the message from Jesus. That is what is major about this book. The early church of A.D. 90

was not concerned about what the American churches 2,000 years into the future thought about their future. The seven churches were consumed by their concern for their own survival. All churches can take comfort that God has declared his concern for his churches over that of any government.

The Faithful Witness

Blessed are those who have been persecuted for the sake of righteousness, for theirs is the kingdom of heaven.

Blessed are you when men revile you, and persecute you, and say all kinds of evil against you falsely, on account of Me.

—Matthew 5:10 & 11

And Cain told Abel his brother. And it came about when they were in the field, that Cain rose up against Abel his brother and killed him.

—Genesis 4:8

1

1

The Vision of Christ

1 The Revelation of Jesus Christ, which God gave Him to show His bond-servants, the things which must shortly take place; and He sent and communicated it by His angel to his bond-servant John,

2 who bore witness to the word of God and to the testimony of Jesus Christ, even to all that he saw.

We are not left to wonder how this letter was written. God gave this Revelation to Jesus, who then gave it to his angel who gave it to John. We don't have to worry that anything is lost in transmission because all of them are trustworthy, even John. John, being human, would be the weak link in this chain; yet even he bears faithful witness to all that he saw. We know that he is a faithful witness, because he wrote a Gospel and three letters that are also in the New Testament. The things in this Revelation must shortly take place—that means it must happen soon.

3 Blessed is he who reads and who hear the words of the prophecy, and heed the things which are written in it; for the time is near.

This is the first of 7 blessings, which goes not only to the one who reads but also the ones he reads to. A reader was an important part of early church worship, because not everyone in the church of that day could read. Notice that the blessing is not just for reading and hearing; to receive the blessing you must also heed the words of the prophecy. There are things in this book that must be obeyed. If this book is for the distant future, a map of the future events, then there is nothing for us to obey because we won't be around then—not to mention the original readers, who have been dead for 1,900 years. Yet if the book is about events that soon will take place because the time is near, not far off as Daniel was told about his book (Daniel 12:4); then the original readers and all subsequent readers, even I must obey the things in this book.

It is a book of Prophecy. Prophecy as we saw in the Introduction calls on what God has said already in his word, applies it to the day and asks why are we not living up to God's Word, and finally as a word about the near future and maybe something of the end of the Age. This prophecy is a near one for he tells us, "the time is near." It is a prophecy for us but not to us; it is to the seven churches of Asia Minor John is writing.

4 John to the seven churches that are in Asia: Grace to you and peace, from Him who is and was and who is to come; and from the seven Spirits who are before His throne;

5 and from Jesus Christ, the faithful witness, the first-born of the dead, and the ruler of the kings of the earth. To Him who loves us, and released us from our sins by his blood.

6 and He has made us to be a kingdom, priests to His God and Father; to Him be the glory and dominion forever and ever Amen.

John writes this letter, which is the Revelation that the Angel got from Jesus who got it from God, to the seven churches. Just as the letters from Paul were written to the Corinthians, yet they are also for us; so this book has information for current situations. We can all learn from it and apply it to our lives. (More about who John is, below in verse 9).

Grace and Peace are greetings we find in the New Testament that come not just from John, but from God Himself. God is the only one who is eternal, He was, He is and He will be. By new Testament times the Jews no longer used the Holy Name of God which had been revealed to Moses. You can't take a name in vain if you never say the Name. So they created a lot of euphemisms for the Living and True God, so they could still talk about him without using His Name. One such euhpemism is "The Eternal One."

The greeting also comes from the Seven Spirits, which, I understand to be the Holy Spirit. Some take the Seven Spirits to be the Seven Angels who stand before the Throne of God. Tradition has even given them the rank of archangels and has named them, but only two appear in the Bible: Michael and Gabriel. Some even suggest these are the seven Angels of the seven churches. These Spirits go out not to Asia Minor, but to all the earth. Seven is the perfect, complete number; therefore the Perfect Spirit, listed with the Father and the Son, I understand to be the Holy Spirit. The flame reminds us not only of the burning bush but also of the tongues of fire seen on the Day of Pentecost.

The Greeting also comes from Jesus Christ. God the Son is described in three ways that help those struggling under persecution.

He is the Faithful Witness. I believe "witness" is a very important word in the Book of Revelation. John is encouraging his readers to be witnesses. The word for witness is *martus/martuia*. From that word we get the word martyr; but that is not the meaning in this book. While it is true that many of the witnesses became martyrs, not all of them did. It is our responsibility to witness, not be martyrs. We are witness when we tell the truth about God and do what we are supposed to do. We are martyrs when others decide to kill us because we will not deny God. Whether or not we become martyrs depends on the evil of others. Whether or not we witness depends on our being faithful. Jesus was faithful. We should be too.

He is the first-born of the dead. If the readers are faithful in their witness there is a good possibility that they could be killed. As a matter of fact they were told that would be a very real possibility. So what. Jesus was also put to death and that did not stop him. If Christians are faithful and find themselves in trouble, we have a Lord who has blazed the trail for us. Death is not the big threat Rome made it out to be. Jesus rose from the dead and so will we.

He is the ruler of the kings of the earth. God gave us governments, Paul tells us in Romans 13, to keep evil men from going too far; but God also judges, and replaces nations. Jesus himself rules the kings of the earth. The government may tell you that you cannot witness, preach, proclaim, pray, or testify; but when they do they overstep their bounds. The answer of the Church has always been that of Peter and John, "Whether it is right in the sight of God to give heed to you rather than to God, you be the judge; for we cannot stop speaking what we have seen and heard." (Acts 4:19-20) Earthly governments sometimes forget that they are not the ultimate authority. It is important for us to remind them as Jesus did to Pilate when Pilate was trying to impress Jesus with his power (just think about that). Jesus said "You have no authority over me, unless it has been given you from above . . . " (John 19:11). In other words: "Pilate, you don't know anything about real power. You've just been given a little power by God, and you will be held accountable for that. God has the ultimate power." And He has commanded His Church to witness.

Who is this Jesus?

He is the one who loves us. John 3:16 tells us that God so loved the world He sent his only begotten son. Jesus said "Greater love has no one than this, that he lay down his life for his friends. You are my friends, if you do what I command" . . . John 15:13–14. But it's not that He loved us and gave His life for us—as great as that is—nor that now He is at the right hand of God the Father making intercession for us (as Hebrews 7:25 tells); but that He *still* loves us. And nothing can separate us from the love of Christ (Romans 8:35–39). No government can take the love of Jesus from us. Now you might say to me I know this stuff, get to the good, exciting things of Revelation. Friend, this *is* the good exciting stuff of Revelation. It just doesn't get any better than the love of Jesus.

He is the one who released us from our sins by His blood. He died to fulfill the law and righteousness and justice of God. He is the sacrifice described in the sacrificial system that was written about in the law. He is the Lamb of God that takes away the sin of the world. He paid the penalty for our sins that we may have fellowship with God. But even more, He released us from the power of sin. Sin no longer has control over of our lives. (Say this sounds more like a study of Romans than Revelation.)

He made us to be a Kingdom of priests to His God. A lot has been written on the Kingdom of God. Jesus spoke about the Kingdom of God in the Gospels, using many parables. And those parables apply to the churches today, for when He spoke of the Kingdom He was talking about those of us who make up the Church. The Kingdom of God is wherever Christ is Lord. We are a kingdom of priests as Peter tells us in his first letter (2:5). If you look for any other Kingdom you are looking for too much.

The mention of God leads properly to a doxology. This is the first of many doxologies.

> 7 Behold, He is coming with the clouds, and every eye will see Him, even those who pierced Him; and all the tribes of earth will mourn over Him. Even so. Amen.

This verse combines thoughts from the Old Testament and the New Testament. Here we see for the first time the way Revelation uses Scripture. Unlike Matthew and Paul who try to establish something from the Old Testament and use proof texts, John only wants to give a feeling from the Old Testament. He's not proving anything, he's revealing something. He's going to take a flavor of this verse and a flavor of that verse and tell you something new.

In Daniel 7:13–14 Daniel is having a dream about the nations to come. He has a vision of God, The Ancient of Days, and then: "I kept looking in the night visions, And behold, with the clouds of heaven One like a Son of Man was coming, And he came up to the Ancient of Days and was presented before Him. And to Him was given dominion, Glory and a kingdom, That all the peoples, nations and men of every language might serve Him. His dominion is an everlasting dominion which will not pass away; And his Kingdom is one which will not be destroyed." While Daniel sees God, Jesus comes into the picture and two things are told about His Kingdom. It will last forever, and it will be made up of all peoples. This is easier for us to understand than it was for Daniel (see Daniel 7:15). We will come back to Daniel 7 often, but for now all we want to see is the Son of Man coming and His people which include all Nations.

8

The other text comes from Zechariah 12:10 "I will pour out on the house of David and on the inhabitants of Jerusalem, the Spirit of grace and of supplication, so that they will look on Me whom they have pierced; and they will mourn for Him, as one mourns for an only son, and they will weep bitterly over Him, like the bitter weeping over a first-born." Here we have the mourning for the one pierced, but in this case the mourners are Jewish. Does this look forward to a day when Jews will be saved, or was this fulfilled by the early Jewish church? Whichever, here we note that those with the Spirit mourn the death of Jesus.

Jesus is coming. He is coming in Judgment. That is a fact, but not what this book is about, for when He comes the problems in this book will be over. No, this statement stands by itself as a truth which all Christians hold dear. Until He comes, we must stand and witness. All we can say to these things is even so, Amen.

8 "I am the Alpha and the Omega," says the Lord God, "who is and was and who is to come, the Almighty."

God Himself signs in at the beginning of this book with a double identity as the Eternal One. This reminds us of Isaiah 41:4 "Who has performed and accomplished it, Calling forth the generations from the beginning? I the Lord am the first, and with the Last. I am He." Alpha and Omega are the first and last letters of the Greek alphabet, which implies that God is first, last and every word in between.

9 I, John, your brother and fellow partaker in the tribulation and kingdom and perseverance which are in Jesus, was on the island called Patmos, because of the word of God and the testimony of Jesus.

I John

We study the lives of Paul and Peter and of course, Jesus, yet the lives of most of the Apostles are a mystery to us. The Bible reveals a lot of information about John, but much of it is in the shadows. This is because in his own Gospel he did not mention his name nor the name of any in his family. Much of what we know of John must come from Matthew, Mark, Luke, Acts, and Corinthians. John did not put his name on his Gospel or on the three letters he wrote. He does identify himself here. In his own Gospel he does not speak of himself, but of another disciple or "the disciple that Jesus loved." There is only one reference to the sons of Zebedee in John. If you assume that John is the other disciple and the disciple that Jesus loved, and if you further assume (as I do) that he wrote all five of the New Testament books attributed to him, then you can put together something of his life (even at that we must qualify some of our findings with "probably" and "it might have been").

John was the son of Zebedee. Zebedee was a man with a fishing business large enough to hire servants; I will leave it to you whether or not that qualifies him to be rich. We know that John had a brother James, who also was a fisherman; and that they were associated with Peter and Andrew, sons of John who were also fishermen. James was probably older because he was mentioned first. We also know that the mother of James and John was in the company of women that followed Jesus. The new thing I found is that many believe that John and Jesus were cousins. By comparing Matt. 27:56 with Mark 15:40 and John 19:25, and assuming that John would not name his natural mother (because he did not name himself or Mary who became his mother at Jesus' death) as well, then we have the very good possibility that

10

Mary's sister is the same as John's mother, therefore making them cousins.

This would put a different light on a lot of things that the Gospels tell about John. For instance there is the request made by John's mother to Jesus that James and John sit at His right and left hands when He comes into the Kingdom (Matt. 20:23). King David had two nephews who were his Generals: Abishi and Joab (2 Samuel 19:43). There would therefore be a precedent set for the Messiah to have two highly placed relatives working in these positions. Yet Jesus pointed out to her she had no idea what she would be asking. As it turned out there were two thieves at his left and right. Jesus asked the two if they would drink the cup He was about to drink, (meaning his suffering and death). Jesus said so you shall, but the Father makes the seating arrangements. John's family ties with Jesus and Mary would also explain not only the boldness of their mother but also the closeness that he enjoyed with them.

Another thing we find out, before Jesus entered his life, was that John was with Andrew, a disciple of John the Baptist (John 1). John the Baptist identified Jesus as the Messiah, and sent the two to follow Jesus. Later James and John were called from their fishing nets as was Peter and Andrew to follow Jesus.

John was a Son of Thunder. Jesus called James and John Boanerges, or Sons of Thunder. Jesus had the same trouble with His two cousins that David did with his nephews, they were hotheads. This issue of being on the right and left hands did not go away. Not only did the mother ask but they themselves asked him more than once (Mark 10:35–45). Jesus was walking along the road one day when the disciples began disputing which of them was the greatest. He turned to ask them what they were talking about, and they were ashamed because they had had this conversation before.

Even in the upper room on the night He was betrayed, this argument came up again. Do you think that the Sons of Thunder were far behind? John came to Jesus and, like Joshua did to Moses (Numbers 11:26–29), John wanted to forbid someone else from copying Jesus' ministry (Luke 9:49). In the same chapter of Luke, Jesus comes through a Samaritan village that would not accept Him. James and John wanted to call down fire, and destroy the village. They were correctly called Sons of Thunder.

John was in the inner circle of the Apostles. When Jesus needed to go somewhere without taking all the twelve, he took Peter, James, and John. Some think He took them because they were more spiritual; I join those who think He took them because they were more volatile. For whatever reason, they were there for the raising of Jairus's daughter (Mark 5:37); the Transfiguration (Mark 9:2); and prayer in Gethsemane. It appears to have been standing procedure to keep Peter, James, and John close, or at least closer than the other twelve.

In the upper room John was with the twelve reclining at the table. They did not sit upright in chairs as we do, but rather reclined on one elbow, leaning on pillows at tables low to the ground. Jesus was talking about the one who would betray Him, and Peter didn't hear all of it. Peter asked John what Jesus said. John then did something very natural, he leaned back onto Jesus and asked Him what He said (John 13:22–27). John was comfortable handling Jesus (I John 1:1).

At the foot of the cross John was with Mary. It was natural to be with Aunt Mary at this time of need. Jesus did a remarkable thing. Jesus had the responsibility, as the eldest child, to take care of His mother. On the cross it appeared that He could not do that any longer. The half brothers of Jesus; James, Joseph, Simon and Judas, did not believe yet and perhaps were not there. John was there and Jesus gave the job to John, which John took as an honor.

John became the son of Mary. Mary lived with John in Ephesus, we are told by Church history, and she died there. In Acts, as John and Peter were walking to the temple they healed a beggar and that drew a crowd. Peter by then knew what to do with a crowd so he preached to them. Peter and John were arrested and tried by the Jewish council (Acts 3 & 4). When Philip preached a sermon in Samaria, Peter and John were sent to see if everything was kosher, so to speak. In Acts 12 we find the Sons of Thunder' promise of being able to drink the cup, put to the test. John's brother James was the first Apostle to be killed for the Word of God and the Testimony of Jesus. James, as a Son of Thunder, thundered the truth of the Gospel in the streets of Jerusalem till He was led away. Herod saw that this pleased the Jews, and arrested Peter with the same intent, but God freed Peter and put an end to Herod. With his own brother killed, John outlived all the other twelve apostles, Paul, James (the half brother of Jesus), and Mary their mother. John knew the cost of discipleship. He, himself, was in exile on a prison island for preaching the Gospel.

Tradition tells us that he lived in Ephesus, and for years taught and preached in the area. There is a legend that he reclaimed a young thief. Another legend is that while in a public bath a gnostic heretic came in. John wrapped his robe around him and got out lest God should strike the building to kill the heretic and John get hurt in the process. John himself took of the cup. Tradition tells us he is the only disciple to die a natural death, but he did not live a natural life. He was a martyr in the way that he always used the word; he was a witness. He witnessed even unto death. Another legend says that as an old man when he could not, because of his age, go to church regularly he would be carried on a bed to church and would only say "My little children: Love one another."

John is our brother in Christ, and in verses 9–11 he tells us of his possession, his position, and his commission.

As a Christian John had a great possession. The first thing John mentions as a fellow partaker is Tribulation. If you were told that when you became a Christian all would be health, wealth, and good times, you were told a lie. Jesus on many occasions told his disciples that following Him would bring tribulation. (Matthew 10:17; 24:9; Luke 21:12; John 15:20, to name just a few). In the Sermon on the Mount Jesus pronounced a blessing for those in Tribulation for the sake of the gospel. Later in his ministry when the crowds got too large and political, He told them "if anyone would follow me let him pick up his cross and follow me." They went home. Suffering is part of what we have in Christ Jesus because we are at war with a sinful world.

The Kingdom of our Lord, and of His Christ is at war with this world and its leaders. Those who await the Kingdom misunderstand; the Kingdom has been here for two thousand years. Jesus and John the Baptist both proclaimed that the Kingdom was at hand. The Kingdom came when Jesus died on the cross and rose from the grave. We who are in Christ Jesus are in the Kingdom. If Jesus is your King then you are in the Kingdom. If you spend all your time looking for a future Kingdom, you may miss this one. Because the Kingdom is at war with the world, we have suffering.

One who is called in a peaceful kingdom such as the Kingdom of God, is at war with a sinful and violent world, and needs perseverance. Fortunately for us, this is a gift of the Holy Spirit. In Galatians, Paul lists patience after love, joy and peace. If you are arrested for the faith and executed you are martyr, but you only have to be faithful a short time. If you are not executed, you have to be faithful for a longer time. To be a consistent witness you need from God's Holy Spirit to grow into you and the Patience of God.

John's position is that he is on the island of Patmos because John would not be still about the Gospel. His answer to Rome had been the same as his answer to the Sanhedrin (Acts 4:19 & 20). "Whether it is right in the sight of God to give heed to you rather than to God, you be the judge; for we cannot stop speaking what we have seen and heard."

10 I was in the spirit on the Lord's day, and I heard behind me a loud voice like the sound of a trumpet . . .

John was in the Spirit; this has been understood to mean that he was in some sort of dream-like state, or trance, so that he could see the vision. A better understanding is that he was obedient to the Spirit and yielded to Him, and in that relationship God the Holy Spirit came upon him in a supernatural way to give him this vision. To be spiritual means to be obedient to God's Spirit, which means obedient to His word. Spiritual does not just mean that you had an emotional experience, but that you are in a relationship with God that requires your obedience.

This happened to John on the Lord's Day. This is the same day Jesus rose from the dead, Sunday.

John received his commission. He heard a voice, like a trumpet. Trumpets were sounded during war, and as a call to worship. Trumpets are clear and loud. Trumpets call the soldiers into battle. His call was to write to the Seven Churches.

11 Saying, "write in a book what you see, and send it to the seven churches: to Ephesus and to Smyrna and to Pergamum and to Thyatira and to Sardis and to Philadelphia and to Laodicea."

15

John is not told to write about the future but just to write what he sees. He shares the vision.

John wrote to seven local churches that were in existence in A.D. 90. Only two of those cities have churches today. I do not believe that these churches represent church ages or that every church is a type of one of these churches. I do believe every church can learn from these churches. They do, I am told, follow a Roman postal route. Like every church addressed in the New Testament, each church has its own problems. Every church and every believer can learn from the good and bad that are recorded in these letters. Every church in New Testament times and since has had individual problem. Every church and every believer can learn from these letters.

12 And I turned to see the voice that was speaking with me. And having turned I saw seven golden lampstands;

John turned to see the voice. Now you can't see a voice but if you are going to have a problem with this you have a long way to go. He turned to see the person who was speaking to him. But what he sees first is not a person but seven golden lampstands. There was a golden lampstand in the Tabernacle, that held seven lamps. It gave light in the Holy Place as you were on your way to the Holy of Holies. We do not have to speculate about what these symbolize. Like most symbols we will be told what these mean.

13 and in the middle of the lampstands one like a son of man, clothed in a robe reaching to the feet, and girded across His breast with a golden girdle.

14 And His head and His hair were white like white wool, like snow; and His eyes were like a flame of fire;

16

15 and His feet were like burnished bronze, when it had been caused to glow in a furnace, and His voice was like the sound of many waters.

16 And in His right hand he held seven stars; and out of His mouth came a sharp two-edged sword; and His face was like the sun shining in its strength.

Among the brightness of the lamps and the shining lampstands, John's eyes can focus on someone, the voice he turned to hear. This brings us back to Daniel 7 as seen above. In Daniel Jesus is the Son of Man, and God is the Ancient of Days. But here Jesus looks like the Ancient of Days. This means that he is also eternal as the Father is, or that He looks like the Father or both. He is called the Son of Man. He has a long robe like the High Priest, because he is our Great High Priest.

His head and hair are white, which show age and wisdom. His eyes don't just take in light, they give out light.

His feet show from the bottom of the robe and show the same metal found in the front of the Tabernacle, where the sacrifices were offered. The polished brass reflects like a mirror, judging all who look at it. Looking in a mirror is a form of Judgment (James 1:21–25). His voice is loud and strong, like water over a waterfall or the waves on the ocean.

In his strong hand are the 7 stars and they will be explained with the lampstands below. Out of his mouth comes a sharp two-edged sword (Isaiah 49:2), which is the word of God. A two-edged sword must be handled carefully because it cuts both ways, (one blade faces you). You can't put your hand on one side and push it, because it will cut your hand. His face is too bright for our eyes, for he is like the sun shining in its full strength.

17

17 And when I saw him I fell at his feet as a dead man. And
he laid His right hand upon me, saying, "Do not be afraid,
I am the first and the last,

John's response is natural and proper. When Jesus was
on earth John handled him (I John 1:1, John 13:25). John
who now sees His Lord in His glory has a different attitude,
an attitude of fear. The fear of God is the Beginning of
Widsom. Jesus handled John and tells him not to be afraid,
too late for that. Jesus is the first and the last. Like the Father
He is also eternal.

18 and the living One; and I was dead, and behold, I am alive
forevermore, and I have the keys of death and of Hades."

Not only is He the first and the last, He is the ever living
one (eternal) who was dead and now is alive, never to die
again. Rome reserved for themselves the right of capital punishment. They could kill but they could not bring back to
Life. Jesus has the keys of death and Hades. He did not give
these keys to anyone. The government can only kill you.
Jesus can bring you back to life or send you to hell.

19 "Write therefore the things which you have seen, and the
things which are, and the things which shall take place after
these things.

John gets his commission to write the vision he sees,
which reflects what is going on when John is writing and
what God will soon do about it.

20 "As for the mystery of the seven stars which you saw in
My right hand, and the seven golden lampstands: the seven
stars are the angels of the seven churches, and the seven
lampstands are the seven churches."

18

The lampstands are the troubled churches who are in trouble with the government. Jesus is not far away, he is walking among the lampstands. Like the High Priest who walks into the Tabernacle with his long robes to inspect the lampstand to see if the oil is supplied, if the wick is trimmed and the light is properly shining in the darkness, Jesus cares for his churches, they are not alone and he has the angels of the churches in his hands.

Who are the angels of the churches? Are they real angels who are messengers to the churches, or overseers, or are they the pastors of the churches? It is hard for some to see pastors as angels. The seven letters in Chapters 2 and 3 are addressed to the Angel of each church, that Jesus holds in his hands. Anyone in his hand is safe; no one can take them out of His hand. (John 10:28)

Now you must let the vision be flexible as in a dream and not so literal that you lose the message. When Jesus put his right hand on John did he have the stars in his hand? Well, of course not, that would have hurt John. Yet did the stars ever leave that protective hand? Of course not.

But I say to you, love your enemies, and pray for those who persecute you.

—Matthew 5:44

Then the king said to Doeg, "You turn around and attack the priests." And Doeg the Edomite turned around and attacked the priests, and he killed that day eighty-five men who wore the linen ephod.

—1 Samuel 22:18

2

Seven Letters to Seven Churches

We come now to the letters to the seven churches. These are individual letters or messages from Jesus to each of the seven churches. I do not believe that they are to all the churches, yet they are *for* all the churches. In the same way, letters to Galatia and Philippi that Paul wrote were to individual churches at a point in time; they are not to us because we did not have the problems of the Galatians, nor have we done the kindness of the Philippians. Yet they are for us because we can learn from their experience. These are seven particular churches at a particular time in history. Individuals are named and spoken about. McDowell points out that the letters do not reflect any church government that will later dominate the churches; and that there is no talk of the Church of Jesus Christ, but rather seven individual churches. (pp. 37–38, McDowell)

Each of the letters follows a pattern (but not doggedly). If there is no reason to condemn it then church receives no condemnation. If there is no reason to praise there is no praise. This is another proof that this is a divine book rather than human, for humans can always find fault (such as Job's friends and the Pharisees Jesus dealt with). The basic pattern is:

1. A command to write to the angel of the church.
2. An identification of Jesus usually connected to Chapter 1.

3. The "I know" passage usually is a condemnation for good works or faithfulness.
4. An accusation.
5. A waning or call to repentance.
6. Promise of the reward.
7. A call for all believers to hear what Jesus says to each church. We are invited by the writer to read mail that is not addressed to us, so that we may learn by it.

One last word of introduction concerns the angel or messenger of each church. These letters seem to be to the church as a whole yet they are addressed to the angel of each church. Could the angel be the pastor, or each angel of a church? It's most likely the pastor, yet that leads to some curious thoughts we will not get into.

Ephesus

1 To the angel of the church of Ephesus writes:

Ephesus was the greatest city of Asia but not the capitol. Its harbor opened up to the west. Its roads led east to the Euphrates as well as north and south. It was therefore the trade center of the area. It was also home to magic and many pagan temples; most famous of all was the Temple of Artemis or Diana; it was their claim to fame and was one of the Seven Wonders of the ancient world. The temple worship involved cult prostitution. The temple also served as the bank for kings and merchants, as well as a place of asylum for fleeing criminals. Ephesus was also the home of Heraclitus, the weeping philosopher who said that the inhabitants of the city were "fit only to be drowned and that the reason why he could never laugh or smile was because he lived amidst such terrible uncleanness." (p. 433 Johnson)

We know more about Ephesus than we do any of the other seven churches. In Acts 18 Paul first comes to Ephesus bringing Priscilla and Aquila. Paul reasoned with the Jews from the Scriptures, in the synagogue, and then left for Jerusalem leaving Priscilla and Aquila there. Apollos came in preaching what he knew but it wasn't the whole story. Priscilla and Aquila helped him understand the way of God more fully and helped him on his way.

When Paul came back to Ephesus he found some disciples who only knew of the Baptism of John (Chapter 19). Paul not only helped them, but for over two years made Ephesus a base to reach all of the province of Asia with the Gospel. The work in Ephesus went so well that those involved with the occult who were saved burned their magic books (worth about 50,000 pieces of silver), and the idol makers rioted to try to save their jobs. After the riot (Chapter 20) Paul went to Greece to raise money for the saints in Jerusalem and check on the churches there. On his way back to Jerusalem he did not want to go to Ephesus because he was on his way to Jerusalem and wanted to be there for Pentecost. So he asked the leaders of Ephesus to meet him in Miletus. There among other things he told them:

"Be on guard for yourselves and for all the flock, among which the Holy Spirit has made you overseers, to shepherd the church of God which He purchased with his own blood.
"I know that after my departure savage wolves will come in among you, not sparing the flock; and from among your own selves men will arise, speaking perverse things, to draw away the disciples after them.
"Therefore be on the alert, remembering that night and day for a period of three years I did not cease to admonish each one with tears.

"And now I commend you to God and to the word of His grace, which is able to build you up and give you the inheritance among all those who are sanctified."

—Acts 20:28–32

History tells us that John himself made Ephesus his home and brought Mary, Jesus' mother, there where she is buried. "In the first years of the second century, Ignatius, bishop of Antioch, wrote his first and longest letter to the Ephesians in which he praises them for their unity and blameless Christian conduct and for living in harmonious love under their bishop, Onesimus." (Ladd, p. 37) The Church grew to be one of the strongest in the world, eclipsed only by Constantinople in the 4th Century. The list of bishops of the Ephesian Church stretches into the 11th Century. In 1308 the City fell to the Turks (Sweet, p. 28) and even the Harbor has left the City. The flow of silt down the river has made the ruins of a once great city sit 6 miles back from the coast. There is no Church there now, nor is there a city.

The One who holds the seven stars in His right hand, the One who walks among the seven golden lampstands, says this:

Jesus is the one who not only has the stars in His hands but has a tight hold on them. No one is able to pluck them out of his hand (John 10:27–29). He is not absent from his church. He walks among them and knows everything about them.

2 I know your deeds and your toil and perseverance, and that you cannot endure evil men, and you put to the test those who call themselves apostles, and they are not, and you found them to be false.

24

3 and you have perseverance and have endured for My name's sake, and have not grown weary.

Jesus knows not only their work, but also their hard work, and the fact that they stay at the hard work. They do not grow weary in well doing. The evil men are morally evil, they may talk the talk but they do not walk the walk. You could not be a leader in the Church of Ephesus if you did not keep your testimony. Nor were the Ephesian believers impressed by impostors.

They have endured persecution and are not ready to quit.

4 But I have this against you, that you have left your first love.

In all their hard work to be right they forgot to be loving (1 Peter 3:15). What is the love they lost? Is it the love for God? Did they no longer value worship? Is it the love for each other? Did they no longer love the fellowship? Or is it the love for the unbeliever? Were they losing their zeal for evangelism? Was it one or all of these? I believe that we are not told which one it is because as we read this we may have a different lack of love than they had. If so we would read that love for God was lacking and our love for each other was lacking we would not be convicted of our sin. It's specific enough for them and vague enough for us.

But is this a big problem? Don't they get a pass for having great theology? How serious is this, really?

5 Remember therefore from where you have fallen, and repent and do the deeds you did at first; or else I am coming to you, and will remove your lampstand out of its place—unless you repent.

This is so serious they could lose it all. Everyone is to know we are Christians by our love. Good theology is always good but everything must be done in love. God is Love. We cannot be Godly and unloving at the same time.

The prescription for this is three-fold. First, remember what it was like when you first trusted Christ and your love was strong. Remember all the things you did without complaint. Remember where you were and compare it with what you are, and see how far you have fallen.

Second, repent from your cold indifference and turn around, go in the opposite direction. Third, do the deeds you did at first. Don't wait till you feel like it, just do it. The feelings will follow the action. Do loving things and you will feel more loving.

6 Yet this you do have, that you hate the deeds of the Nicolaitans, which I also hate.

Now after being in trouble for not being loving, Jesus praises them for hating. This helps us understand what love is. Love is not a quivering feeling that makes one a doormat for every bully or open to every idea that comes along. Love is not agreeing all the time or going along with anything. Love must be tough, to be true love. If you love someone you must hate that which stands in opposition to him.

If you love truth you must hate lies. "However, the Ephesian Christians hated what Christ hated without loving those whom he loved." (Robbins p. 57). Jesus does not condemn the Ephesian Church for being too orthodox. Jesus praises them for their stand for the truth. He hates lies also.

We will get into more detail about the Nicolaitans when we get to Pergamum. Here let us see that love does not mean that you are wishy-washy and you believe all ideas and deeds are of equal value.

7 "He who has an ear, let him hear what the Spirit says to the churches. To him who overcomes, I will grant to eat of the tree of life, which is in the Paradise of God."

The Tree of Life was in the Garden of Eden. It was not the forbidden tree. The forbidden tree was the Tree of Knowledge of Good and Evil. Once our parents ate of that tree it was important to get them out of the garden away from the Tree of Life. What if they ate of the Tree of Life and lived forever in sin? They had to get out of Eden to get forgiveness. The Tree of Life is a symbol of the Cross of Jesus, as we shall see in Chapter 22.

"Behold, I send you out as sheep in the midst of wolves; therefore be shrewd as serpents, and innocent as doves."

—Matthew 10:16

Now Ahab called Obadiah who was over the household. (Now Obadiah feared the LORD greatly; for it came about, when Jezebel destroyed the prophets of the LORD, that Obadiah took a hundred prophets and hid them by fifties in a cave, and provided them with bread and water.)

—1 Kings 18:3–4

Smyrna

8. "And to the angel of the Church of Smyrna write:

Smyrna is a smaller town than Ephesus, about forty miles north, although it rivaled Ephesus as a seaport and city of commerce. It was destroyed by fire about 295 B.C., and had to be completely rebuilt. Therefore it was one of the most planned cities in the ancient world. Smyrna claimed to be the birthplace of Homer. It was the first city to worship the goddess Roma, and was loyal to Rome even before it was a world power. It did win from "the Roman senate in A.D. 23 (over eleven other cities) the privilege of building the first temple in honor of Tiberius." (Newport p. 146) Johnson reports that under Domitian, emperor worship became compulsory for every Roman citizen on threat of death and quotes Barclay that one would get a certificate to prove the worship was carried out. (Johnson p. 437)

> The most famous martyrdom of the early church fathers was that of the elderly Polycarp, the 'twelfth martyr in Smyrna,' who, upon his refusal to acknowledge Caesar as Lord, was placed upon a pyre to be burned.
>
> —(Mounce, p. 91)

Many believe that Polycarp was the Bishop of Smyrna at this time. We know that he was a Christian at this time and eventually he became the bishop, but we have no record of exactly who was bishop at the time Revelation was written. He was no doubt a church member in training. In A.D. 115, twenty years after Revelation, Ignatius wrote to the church at Smyrna and its Bishop Polycarp. (Beasley-Murray p. 80)

Smyrna is the only one of the seven cities still in existence (modern Izmir). In the first century Smyrna, Pergamum, and Ephesus were in competition for first city of Asia.

29

While Ephesus has lost its harbor, Smyrna's is just fine, thank you very much. "Through the centuries it has remained a strong Christian witness and is today one of the great centers of piety and learning of the Orthodox church. The Muslims call is the 'Infidel City' because of its Christian witness. Ramsay calls it the "City of Life.' Some scholars think that this is the oldest continuous Christian witness in the church. (Robbins p. 58).

The first and the last, who was dead, and has come to life, says this: As Smyrna strove to be first against other cities, Jesus is First; and not only that, He is the Last. He was dead; therefore we have no reason to fear death. Jesus has been there, done that, got the T-shirt. Death is not the big deal the Romans make it out to be, if you trust in Him. After death is the Judgment, and if you believe in Jesus he has taken the Judgment for you. Jesus was dead but now he lives forever more. For the believer all we hope for lies beyond death, because Jesus took the fear out of it.

9. I know your tribulation and your poverty (but you are rich), and the blasphemy by those who say they are Jews and are not, but are a synagogue of Satan.

The word for tribulation is the word for pressure. G. Campbell Morgan said, "Our word tribulation suggests the stripe of the Roman whip, but the word that the Master used, suggested rather the pressure of the stones that grind the wheat, or that force the blood out of the grape. It is a word that throbs with meaning. These people were being pressed even to death on account of their loyalty to Christ, and as He looks at the church, He says in tones of infinite tenderness, I know thy tribulation." (Morgan, p. 60)

Jesus also knows their poverty. Christians, all things being equal, should not live in poverty because they can read

Proverbs (as did Calvin) and work hard for their living as Paul did (1 Thessalonians 2:9). But all things are not equal. These Christians lived in a pro-Roman city, in a time when emperor worship was mandatory, that had a large Jewish community that was hostile to Christians. If they could get work, and work at low wages, they would still be poor—but they could not get work. Today we would use the word discrimination. This word is below that; they cannot get work. And no doubt hate-filled mobs came by and robbed them of the little they did have. They are poor in the things of this world but rich toward God. The bank account they have in Heaven makes them very rich (Matthew 6:19–21).

The slander against His church, Jesus calls blasphemy. That blasphemy is done by a group that should be known as the Lord's congregation; instead they are the synagogue of Satan. Jesus did not say this because it is Christian to be anti-Semitic. It is not. Half of the church in Smyrna, John and Jesus were all Jewish. Jesus told the woman at the well that Salvation is of the Jews (John 4:22). Nor is He saying this because true Jews are Jews in spirit (Romans 2:28–29), and those who reject Jesus deserve this title, as Ladd suggests (Ladd, p. 44). It's not just that they reject Jesus but that they go farther and attack Christians (John 8:31–47).

It is because they do the work of Satan who is our adversary (in the Hebrew meaning of the word) and slanders (in the Greek) the church of God. It is the outward work of hate that earns them this title. The same thing could be said of a supposed Christian congregation who joined with Hitler to exterminate the Jews. In the martyrdom of Polycarp, when he was about to be burned at the stake Jews helped gather the wood even though it was the Sabbath.

10. Do not fear what you are about to suffer. Behold, the devil is about to cast some of you into prison, that you may

be tested, and you will have tribulation ten days. Be faithful until death, and I will give you the crown of life.

"Do not fear," is usually said in the Bible when an angel appears to someone, and he usually says it too late. The angel would appear, the person would be afraid, and the angel would say, "Fear not;" meaning, I'm not going to hurt you. No harm will come to you. It does not mean that here. Harm is to come and you are not to fear it.

The hatred does not come from Rome, Jews, or Smyrna, it comes from the devil. He has been given permission to put some of you in prison, a place you go to await trial or death.

There is much comment on what the ten days mean. Numbers in Revelation are symbolic. Summers sees the ten days to mean complete tribulation. A translatable possibility is that the tribulation is within ten days. Others see the number 10 as symbolic—meaning a short time that seems a long time when you're in it. I have lived most of my life in Southern California, and I can tell you 10 seconds of an earthquake is a long time. The time has an end to it, and God knows that it is going to happen and when it is going to stop.

"Faithful" should be "trustworthy," according to Sweet. As the city is faithful to Rome, the church is to be more faithful to Jesus. Death has been defeated and is not the end. Nor is it any longer to be feared.

11. He who has an ear, let him hear what the Spirit says to the churches. He who overcomes shall not be hurt by the second death.

"The second death is a Rabbinic term for the death of the wicked in the next world" (Mounce, p. 94). Till Jesus comes back death is still one to a customer, whether you are a Christian or not. If you are a Christian, you have a second birth and you only die once. If you reject Jesus as Lord you will die twice. If Jesus is your Lord you will be faithful unto death.

Fear not them which kill the body, but are not able
to kill the soul: but rather fear him which is able to
destroy both soul and body in Hell.

—Matthew 10:28

Eleazar, one of the scribes in high position, a man
now advanced in age and of noble presence, was being
forced to open his mouth to eat swine's flesh. But he,
welcoming death with honor rather than life with pollu-
tion, went up to the rack of his own accord, spitting
out the flesh, as men ought to do who have the courage
to refuse things that are not right to taste even for the
natural love of life.

I beseech you, my child, to look at the heaven and
the earth and see everything that is in them and recognize that God did not make them out of things that
existed. Thus also mankind comes into being. Do not
fear this butcher, but prove worthy of your brothers.
Accept death, so that in God's mercy I may get you back
again with your brothers . . . So he died in his integrity,
putting his whole trust in the Lord. Last of all the
mother died, after her (seven) sons.

—2 Maccabees 6:18–20; 7:28–29, 40–41

Pergamum

12 And to the angel of the church in Pergamum write:

From Smyrna you take the coast road up about 40 miles then turn northeast up the Caicus Valley to the capitol of the Asian Roman province, Pergamum. Unlike Ephesus and Smyrna, Pergamum did not have a harbor nor was it on a major trade road. It did have the Roman Governor. Governors were divided by which one could wield the sword or not (which ones had the power of capital punishment). Pergamum had the sword.

The One who has the sharp two-edged sword says this:

Another reminder to the church that whatever power Rome claimed to have, its power is really from God. It is God that has the ultimate power. The sword is an interesting instrument of God's wrath. We think of the sword as something man made for warfare, but have you ever thought about where the first sword appears? Genesis 3:24 records that the first sword is a flaming sword in the hands of the cherubim who kept man from the Garden. The sword represents the judgment of God, and is given to worldly governments to rule in the place of God, to be an avenger of wrath upon the one who practices evil (Romans 13:1–7). The Church is to proclaim the Gospel; the State is to punish evil in the world. Ultimate Judgment belongs to Jesus who will judge not only churches but also states.

13 I know where you dwell, where Satan's throne is; and you hold fast My name, and did not deny My faith, even in the days of Antipas, My witness, My faithful one, who was killed among you, where Satan dwells.

There were many reasons to understand that Satan dwelt in this city. The Temple to Zeus up on the hill looked like a throne. There were temples to other gods, such as healing gods that took the symbol of a snake. Josephus even tells us of a Jewish Synagogue, yet it is not the problem it is in other cities.

There are two armrests of Satan's throne. The temple of Rome and Augustus, and the seat of the Governor, ensured that emperor worship was strictly enforced. To be a loyal citizen, one must burn incense to Caesar and say "Caesar is Lord."

Christians could not do this. To do this would deny the name of Jesus as Lord. Even when Antipas lost his life rather than worship Caesar, the rest of the church held fast to Jesus.

> 14 But I have a few things against you, because you have there some who hold the teaching of Balaam, who kept teaching Balak to put a stumbling block before the sons of Israel, to eat things sacrificed to idols, and to commit acts of immorality.

There are a few in the church, however, who are showing signs of weakness in this area. They hold to the teaching of Balaam who was hired by Balak, the King of Moab, to curse Israel when Moses was bringing them up from Egypt. Balaam was a prophet with a great reputation (Numbers 22–24) for speaking for God. Balak had a lot of gold to give him if Balaam was successful. Balaam was a prophet for profit, but he could not curse Israel because he was a true prophet; every time he opened his mouth blessings would come out. He failed. But rather than see all that money get away he said to Balak, "Listen, if you want God to curse these people all you have to do is cause them to sin. Bring your temple prostitutes and idols and under a white flag go out and meet them. Cause them to sin and God will curse them (Numbers 31:13–20). That worked.

In Pergamum you had a group within the church that began to say, "What's the big deal? If they force me to say things against my will it's not the real me doing it. What the flesh does is not as important as the spirit. If I in my flesh eat meat at a festival, I'm still saved. There is no reason to be so narrow and judgmental." Compromise with sin had gotten Jesus's attention. In Ephesus Jesus hated this doctrine, and he didn't like it any better in the capitol.

15 Thus you have some who in the same way hold the teaching of the Nicolaitans.

It's not clear whether the Balaamites are the same as the Nicolaitans or they just share an antinomian creed. Two bad apples in this barrel are enough.

16 Repeat therefore; or else I am coming to you quickly and I will make war against them with the sword of My mouth.

This coming quickly is not the same as other such statements in Revelation, this is not for the second coming. This is for a more personal visit to fix a problem He has in His Church. Today the sharp two-edged sword is available to us to take care of anyone teaching such compromise with the world.

17 He who has an ear, let him hear what the Spirit says to the churches. To him who overcomes, to him I will give some of the hidden manna, and I will give him a white stone, and a new name written on the stone which no one knows but he who receives it.

Everyone needs to hear that God's Spirit does not like his people compromising with sin. When Moses brought the people out of Egypt, manna fell from heaven. Moses took some of it and put it in a special jar, and put that in the Ark. By the time of Solomon that jar was gone. (1 Kings 8:9) Jeremiah couldn't (as some suggest) take away the jar; it was not there to take away by his time. The manna speaks of Jesus and his sustenance of our salvation. It even speaks of the Lord's Supper. Much has been written about the white stone. "The white stone was associated with and was used as a symbol of hospitality, friendship, acquittal, public honor, admission ticket, a happy day, a dole ticket, token of victory, token of nobility, and an amulet." (Robbins, p. 65) Others see a Diamond, or Christ; still others see the Urim and Thummim. All these have implications for believers. The new name is exciting because we do not know if it is a name for God, or Jesus, or the believer. It is personal for each believer and it speaks of that special relationship between Jesus and the one who overcomes.

Woe to you, scribes and Pharisees, hypocrites! For you build the tombs of the prophets and adorn the monuments of the righteous, and say, "If we had been living in the days of our fathers, we would not have been partners with them in shedding the blood of the prophets."

Consequently you bear witness against yourselves, that you are the sons of those who murdered the prophets.

Fill up then the measure of the guilt of your fathers.

You serpents, you brood of vipers, how shall you escape the sentence of hell?

Therefore, behold, I am sending you prophets and wise men and scribes; some of them you will kill and crucify, and some of them you will scourge in your synagogues, and persecute from city to city,

that upon you may fall the guilt of all the righteous blood shed on earth, from the blood of righteous Abel to the blood of Zechariah, the son of Berechiah, whom you murdered between the temple and the altar.

—Matthew 23:29–35

Thyatira

18 And to the angel of the church in Thyatira write:

Forty miles southeast of Pergamum is Thyatira, not as large as the other cities we have seen so far; in fact it is called the least of all the cities, but it has the largest letter from Jesus. It lies in the valley that connects the two valleys of Hermus and the Caicus. Thus it becomes a trade center, between the two. (Barclay, p. 101)

It has no emperor worship, but it does have a lot of labor guilds, and each "guild had its own patron deity, feasts, and seasonal festivities that include sexual revelries." (Johnson, p. 443) Morris quotes Sir William Ramsay listing the trade guilds as "wool-workers, linen-workers, makers of outer garments, dyers, leather-workers, tanners, potters, bakers, slave-dealers and bronze-smiths." (Morris, pp. 69–70). If you had a job or a skill it was expected that you take part in the food sacrificed to the idol of your profession, and if it was the right time of the year the festival would lead to sexual immorality.

Lydia, the seller of purple that Paul met in Philippi (Acts 16:14), was from here. She left Thyatira to sell the purple garments of Thyatira and we have no record of her returning home.

There are a lot of allusions in this letter to Psalm 2. It might be good just to stop here and read the second Psalm before continuing.

The Son of God, who has eyes like a flame of fire, and His feet are like burnished bronze, says this: The Son of God is a title we use in the Church all the time, but is very sparingly used. It is used in Psalm 2. He has the eyes that penetrate the heart and minds of men.

The feet of bronze ; "feet as brass refined in service" (Summers, p. 117) speak of Judgment. In the Tabernacle that Moses built all the articles outside which could be seen by the people were bronze. Bronze reflects your image like a mirror; in fact, early mirrors were bronze. Nothing is more judgmental than a mirror. Outside the tabernacle is where Israel dealt with its sins, at the brazen altar and the brazen laver where the priests washed between each service. The effect of one whose eyes give out light instead of taking in light, and whose feet can stomp anyone, make him a fearful King.

19 I know your deeds, and your love and faith and service and perseverance, and that your deeds of late are greater than at first.

The order of this verse has four "deeds" and three "yours." The "Yours" separate the sections of the verse. He knows their deeds. He lists their deeds. He judges the progress of their deeds.

Love, like in the letter of Ephesus, is not spelled out as to what kind of love it is; or to whom, God or man or both. Whatever Epesus did not have, Thyatira did.

Faith is not, as some have said, faithfulness which is a part of their faith; but it is the faith once for all delivered to the saints (Jude 3). The problem with this church is not that they had bad theology, but that they tolerated someone with bad theology.

Service: Linsky makes a distinction between slaves (douloi) and servants (diakonia), being voluntary. He says "At the wedding of Cana we find diakonoi, because they served freely. Mary who managed things found it necessary to tell them to do what Jesus would say lest they follow their own free ideas and think it foolish to do what this guest might say. Douloi are slaves whose sole business is to obey. Diakonia is the service we render to our brethren . . . '' (Linsky, p. 114) You may be familiar with that word, diakonia. That's where we get the word "deacon;" it means service.

Perseverance: is the ability to not grow weary in well-doing. The Christian life is not that you do good once; but because of God working in you, you do more often till it becomes a habit, or a life-style.

These four deeds of the church did not slack off as they did in Ephesus. The Church in Thyatira grew in Grace.

> 20 But I have this against you, that you tolerate the woman Jezebel who calls herself a prophetess, and she teaches and leads My bond-servants astray, so that they commit acts of immorality and eat things sacrificed to idols.

Jezebel (not her real name) is some woman teaching in the church as a prophetess, teaching immorality as her namesake did in the Old Testament (1 Kings 16:31ff; 2 Kings 9:22). Who is this Jezebel? Some have suggested the fortune teller that lived just out of town called the Sambathe who gave out oracles, one of the few things we know about Thyatira's religion. This is dismissed because she is obviously a member of the Church. A second idea is that she is the pastor's wife. This comes from a less reliable manuscript, yet the thought is interesting. Hobbs says it's "a family-controlled church, dominated by this woman Jezebel." (Hobbs, p. 49) Barclay says "That would be an interesting sidelight on the early Christian congregations and it would not be the last time that the wives of church officials were the sources of trouble in a congregation." (Barclay, p. 104) Perhaps some unmarried scholar can work on this angle; we will follow the preferred reading and not let our minds wander on our own experiences.

Whoever this Jezebel was, she enjoyed the festivals of the city and did not feel that becoming a Christian should mean that all the fun should stop. You could lose business if you didn't go to the feasts and participate. Later, we know that people taught that what you did with your body did not affect your soul. How can you experience grace if you do not experience the "deep things" of this world? You can have it all.

> 21 And I gave her time to repent; and she does not want to repent of her immorality.

God by his grace gives us time to repent. The reason some people still breathe in and out is that God is giving them time to repent. The world says that if there is a God why does he not do something about evil? He will, He is just giving you a chance to repent.

That she does not repent means she has rejected God's offer of grace. The God of Heaven comes to earth and takes on our sin and gives his life for us and people say "no thanks, I don't need it." They have contempt for the grace of God and God has contempt for them. She does not even want to repent. Only a God who can see into the hearts and minds can know this. (Morgan, p. 124)

> 22 Behold, I will cast her upon a bed of sickness, and those who commit adultery with her into great tribulation, unless they repent of her deeds.

Suggestions on what cast her upon a bed have been: a bed for resting, for guild-banqueting, for sickness, for death (as a funeral bier). The text just says "cast her upon a bed," but Beasley-Murray says this is a "Hebraistic expression for becoming ill." (Beasley Murray, p. 91) Whatever it means this time she is thrown onto the bed against her will, and into tribulation with those she has led.

Unless, of course, they repent. Prophecy is also a means of the grace of God, to warn people of the Judgment to come. If they repent, God will forgive; the Judgment can be delayed, or stopped altogether. Even King Ahab, the wicked husband of the real Jezebel, turned back the wrath of God once (1 Kings 21:27–29). "God is not willing that any should perish but that all come to repentance." 2 Peter 3:9.

> 23 And I will kill her children with pestilence; and all the churches will know that I am He who searches the minds and hearts; and I will give to each one of you according to your deeds.

"I will kill her children;" most commentators take this to mean her followers; but wouldn't that be the ones spoken of in verse 22? We don't like a God who kills children—however, we don't get to shop around for gods. There is only one God and we have better learn to deal with the one we have. The real Jezebel lost all her children to a violent death. So did King Jeroboam I of Israel (1 Kings 14:7–16), and many others. Exodus 20:5 tells us that the children of idolators suffer for the sins of their fathers. This is a hard saying and we need to understand some things:

1. God is sovereign, and does not have to save any of us. God can do whatever He wants. He is God.
2. Children are not innocent, according to Psalm 51:5.
3. The worst thing that could happen to you is not that you die, but that you continue to live in sin.
4. God loves children more than anyone on earth (Matthew 18:1–10), even more than the atheist who uses suffering children to accuse God when they ought to accuse the adults that cause the children to suffer. We know God will.

God is not the bad guy here, Jezebel is. She will not repent even when her children's lives are on the line. "I will kill them," the Greek says literally, "with death." That should do the job. "I will kill them with death." Could this be a reference to the second death? Newport translates "I will strike her children dead" then suggests it might be a Hebrew idiom denoting "pestilence." (Newport, p. 153) Mounce quotes Moffatt and says it is a Hebraism that means "to slay utterly," then backs off and prefers "To kill by pestilence." (Mounce, p. 105)

The heart and mind (Jeremiah 11:20) are open to God. "Jezebel's sins pollute the mind, ruin the body, destroy the conscience, and paralyze the will of those who practice them." (Robbins p. 68)

24 But I say to you, the rest who are in Thyatira, who do not hold this teaching, who have not known the deep things of Satan, as they call them—I place no other burden on you.

The rest of the people in the church did not hold to the teaching of Jezebel. They do not know the "deep things," nor did they want to know. They thought this might be wrong but now they know they must distance the church from this false prophetess. How you live and what you do with your body makes a difference.

In Acts 15 the early church came together in Jerusalem because they had a problem. Christianity was a Jewish religion and everyone understood how to practice it but then Gentiles came to know Jesus and the question was do they now need to become Jews? We find the answer (no) in Paul's letter to the Galatians and in Acts 15 where the Jerusalem Church is led by James, the half-brother of the Lord.

Ladd points out that the words "no other burden" come from that letter James sent by Paul, where the church asked Gentile believers not to eat things offered to idols and fornication (Acts 15) (Ladd p. 53). Jesus is asking why after so many years the followers of Jezebel are not keeping the agreement?

25 Nevertheless what you have, hold fast until I come.

What do they have but "the sum total of Christian doctrine and hope and privilege" (Alford, p. 577).

26 And he who overcomes, and he who keeps My deeds until the end, TO HIM I WILL GIVE AUTHORITY OVER THE NATIONS.

AND HE SHALL RULE THEM WITH A ROD OF IRON, AS THE VESSELS OF THE POTTER ARE BROKEN TO PIECES, as I also have received authority from My Father;

This also comes from Psalm 2. As the Son of God has authority, so he gives it to his church. The enemies of the church will be shattered. Go forth to the battle and be fearless.

"The smashing of earthen pots in places is another symbol of universal power. It is derived from a custom of Egyptian and Mesopotamian kings, in coronation rituals, who would publicly smash pottery vessels on which the names of their enemies, or of all other nations, had been inscribed." (Ashcraft, p. 270)

"The conqueror is promised that he will share the functions of the Messiah himself: 'You shall break them with a rod of iron, and dash them in pieces like a potter's vessel' (Ps. 2:9). This phrase is repeated in the vision of the coming of Christ . . . A problem occurs in the Greek text for the word in the Septuagint which translates the Hebrew. 'To break' or 'shatter' is a word which means basically 'to tend a flock' and often has the idea of ruling in the sense of protection and preserving (see Matt. 2:6; John 21:16; Rev. 7:17).'' (Ladd, p. 54) When we think of shepherding we think of the peaceful waters, lush grass and peaceful scenery of Psalm 23. We forget that the valley of the Shadow of Death is also in that psalm. We also forget David's experience with the lion and the bear (1 Samuel 17:34–36). Shepherding the flock of God in an evil world is war. "At Thyatira the battle was to be won by resolute adherence to the 'works of Christ,' i.e. to the purity of the Christian life as opposed to the 'works of Jezebel.' " (Sweet. p. 46)

28 and I will give him the morning star.

The morning star is Venus. Lohmeyeer (E. Lohmeyer *Die Offenbarung des Johannes,* Handbuch zum Neuen Testament, Tubingen 2nd edn,1953) has shown that from Babylonian times Venus was the symbol of sovereignty. In Roman times it was more specifically the symbol of victory and sovereignty . . . " (Beasley-Murray p. 93). (Daniel 12:3; 2 Peter 1:19)

One who has frequently observed the brilliant beauty of the morning star in the dark hour which precedes the dawn will understand the beauty of this promise. He may often walk in darkness and in many perplexities, but the morning star will be given to guide him; he must refuse to follow the false leadership of gnosticism and wait for the star." (Summers, p. 119) In Rev. 22:16 Jesus is the morning star. What more could a Christian ask for?

In the first three letters the "He who has an ear" came before the prize to the victor; in the last four it serves as a warning and benediction.

29 He who has an ear, let him hear what the Spirit says to the churches.

But Jesus answered and said, "You do not know what you are asking for. Are you able to drink the cup that I am about to drink?" They said to Him, "We are able."

He said to them, "My cup you shall drink; but to sit on My right and on My left, this is not Mine to give, but it is for those for whom it has been prepared by My Father."

—Matthew 20:22–23

And having been prompted by her mother, she said, "Give me here on a platter the head of John the Baptist."

And although he was grieved, the king commanded it to be given because of his oaths, and because of his dinner guests.

And he sent and had John beheaded in the prison.

—Matthew 14:8–10

3

Sardis

1 And to the angel of the church in Sardis write:

Continuing southeast on the postal road we come to Sardis, about 30 miles from Thyatira. It was known as the place where dyed woolen garments came from, but its real glory is in its past. In the 6th century B.C. it was the capitol of the ancient kingdom of Lydia, with its King Croesus (from which we derive the phrase "rich as Croesus"). "Croesus embarked upon a war with Cyrus of Persia which was the end of the greatness of Sardis . . . To get at the armies of Cyrus he had to cross the River Halys. He took counsel of the famous oracle at Delphi and was told: 'If you cross the River Halys, you will destroy a great empire.' " (Barclay, p. 114) He thought they meant the Persian empire and not his own.

Sardis was built on a steep northern spur of Mt. Tmolus and was essentially inaccessible to invading armies. But twice the city fell because the defenders were so secure that they did not watch at night, and did not see the few soldiers climb up cliffs to unlock the gate. The city fell twice because they were asleep. As the years went by and the city grew, not everyone could fit on the top of the mountain, so Sardis became two cities one above and one below.

"The people of the city were widely known for their luxurious, loose way of life. It is significant that nothing is said in the letter about Jewish hostility, about open persecution, or about heretical teaching. The main problem is that of a deep spiritual apathy, which may have resulted from the softness and love of luxury which characterized the secular society." (Ladd, p. 55).

> He who has the seven Spirits of God, and the seven stars, says this: I know your deeds, that you have a name, that you are alive, and you are dead.

Jesus identifies himself as the One who holds the seven stars, the angels of the Churches, and the seven Spirits of God which are symbolic of the Holy Spirit. A person is dead when he no longer responds to God or the people around him. A church is dead when it no longer responds to the Holy Spirit. It's a body cut off from the head.

Jesus says "I know" and in the other letters says the good things about the church. The only possible good thing he has to say about Sardis is that they have great public relations. In our modern times there was a manufacturing company that had as its motto, "The quality goes in before the name goes on." In the case of Sardis, the name went on after the quality was gone. This is the worst thing you can say about a church. It is not about the theology, or anything else that the other churches deal with; it is about the fact that this organization that seems alive to everyone else is dead to God. This is a church at one with the community in which it lives. It does not offend the pagans around it. When sinners come in they are right at home. The Gospel does not offended because they rarely (if ever) hear it.

> 2 Wake up, and strengthen the things that remain, which were about to die; for I have not found your deeds completed in the sight of My God.

The good news is that there are things that remain. The church has a few weak signs of life. She needs to wake up before the enemy climbs the wall again and destroys the church totally.

In the lower city was an incomplete Temple to the Asiatic goddess of Cybele (the Greek Artemis, or Roman Diana, the goddess of sex). "This patron deity was believed to possess the special power of restoring the dead to life." (Mounce, p. 109) Just as that temple lay unfinished so did the deeds of love, faith, service, and patience that Jesus looks for in his churches. There was a start, but no followthrough.

3 Remember therefore what you have received and heard; and keep it, and repent. If therefore you will not wake up, I will come like a thief, and you will not know at what hour I will come upon you.

Remember the gospel you have received. Get back to the basics of what you are supposed to believe. When a sports team is losing they go back over the fundamentals that they learned as children first playing the game. When a musician is having problems with some piece of music he will go over and over the same piece, or go back over the scales that he learned when he first started, until he has got it right. When a church is almost dead—or before that happens—they need to examine themselves and the Scriptures, and see if they have it right.

Am I living the gospel? Before I go to anyone else I examine myself and I must adjust myself. I must remember the time I came to Christ and, in the same way, now come to him in repentance and submission (Colossians 2:6). Then I need to walk in a different way to prove the grace of God has saved me from my sin. I can no longer live like the world. The problem with this church is that they did not live differently than those around them. Those around them were partaking in orgies as a part of pagan worship.

51

Again Jesus says He will come to a church for judgment. Jesus is coming again but this is not His second coming, this is a visitation to that church to bury the dead.

When Jesus comes again no one will know when. Thieves do not make reservations, or appointments; in fact, they do not want you to know when they come. When Jesus comes He does not want you to know; you will wait and then prepare. He is coming at a time when you think not.

4 But you have a few people in Sardis who have not soiled their garments; and they will walk with Me in white, for they are worthy.

There are a few people (lit. names) who have not soiled their garments. They do not worship sex, and live like the world. God has always had a faithful few. They will walk with Jesus in bright clothing, not just white but glowing.

They are worthy because Jesus made them worthy by dying on the cross for their sins. We know they are saved because they live like it. They walk with God on earth and they will walk with God in heaven.

5 He who overcomes shall thus be clothed in white garments; and I will not erase his name from the book of life, and I will confess his name before My Father, and before His angels.

The victorious one shall have three things happen to him. First, he will be clothed in white. Mounce notes that there are 7 times we are told the righteous wear white. (3:4, 3:5, 3:18, 4:4, 7:9, 7:13, 19:14, Mounce p. 113) The white clothes are said to mean: Festivity, Justification, Resurrection, Triumph, but most likely Purity.

Second, God will not erase his name from the Book of Life. Moses first tells us about the Book of Life when he argues with God about it. (Ex. 32:32; also see Ps. 60:28, Isa. 4:3, Dan. 12:1, Luke 10:20, Phil. 4:3, Heb. 12:23, Rev. 13:8, 17:8, 20:12, 20:15, 21:27) Cities used to keep a record of their citizens who were alive. If you moved, died, or committed treason or some other major crime against the city, your name might be blotted out. Those who trust Him never have to worry about that.

Last, Jesus will confess your name before the Father and the Angels. Jesus has said this many times. (Matt. 10:32, Luke 12:8)

6 'He who has an ear, let him hear what the Spirit says to the churches.'

Then they will deliver you up to Tribulation, and will kill you, and you will be hated by all nations on account of My name.

—Matthew 24:9

. . . and he said, "Behold, I see the Heavens opened up and the Son of Man standing at the right hand of God."

But they cried out with a loud voice, and covered their ears, and they rushed upon him with one impulse.

And when they had driven him out of the city, they began stoning him, and the witnesses laid aside their robes at the feet of a young man named Saul.

And they want on stoning Stephen as he called upon the Lord and said, "Lord Jesus, receive my spirit!"

And falling on his knees, he cried out with a loud voice, "Lord, do not hold this sin against them!" And having said this, he fell asleep.

—Acts 7:56–60

Philadelphia

And to the angel of the church in Philadelphia write:

Continuing on our postal road: twenty-five miles southeast of Sardis is the youngest of the seven cities—Philadelphia, the city of brotherly love. It was named after Attalus II who loved his brother Eumenes and founded the city in the second century B.C. It was founded near the border of Lydia and Phrygia for the purpose of spreading the Greek culture to these areas. It was a missionary city before Christianity came to the area. Like the other seven cities, Philadelphia sits on an earthquake belt. The earthquake of A.D. 17 devastated many cities in the area overnight and Roman money had to be sent to rebuild. It is also the sight of volcanic activity and hot springs. Although many gods are worshiped, Dionysus was the chief god of the area because of all the wine produced there.

He who is holy, who is true, who has the key of David, who opens and no one will shut, and who shuts and no one opens says this:

The identification of Jesus is not confined to the discriptions in Chapter one. Only God is Holy. Only God is True (Habakkuk 3:3, Isaiah 40:25, Revelation 6:10). Jesus is God, and He has the key of David. The church is having trouble with the Jewish Synagogue in town saying that the Jewish believers are not real Jews and persecuting the church. Jesus departs from the opening to say he not only has the keys of death, (those who face death need to know that), He also has the keys of David. As Messiah He sits on David's throne; and you do not get any more Jewish than that (Isaiah 22:22).

8 I know your deeds. Behold, I have put before you an open door which no one can shut, because you have a little power, and have kept My word, and have not denied My name.

Jesus gives them an open door which no man can shut. The door of the Synagogue had been shut on them but now Jesus opens not only that door so that more Jews can come to know Jesus or Messiah, but other doors as well. Paul told the Corinthians that he could not come to them for a while because a wide door for effective service had opened in Ephesus. When Jesus opens a door for us no man can shut it, but do we see it? Will we go through it? God gives us opportunities—but do we use them?

Jesus says, "I know you have a little power . . . " The Synagogue no doubt has more power, and the civil authorities have even more power. Jesus does not condemn them for being small, or tell them that if they don't grow He will have to shut the doors. That they have just a little power or strength is a mere statement of fact that Jesus acknowledges. But even though they are small in power they are not intimidated. They have kept His word and not denied His name as others put pressure on them.

9 Behold, I will cause those of the synagogue of Satan, who say that they are Jews, and are not, but lie—behold, I will make them to come and bow down at your feet, and to know that I have loved you.

As in Smyrna, we meet another synagogue of Satan. There were synagogues in most if not all the cities yet only these two receive this title. Again, it is not that they reject Jesus (they will be judged for that also), but that they do Satan's work rather than the work of Abraham (John 8:39–44). Some want to blame John for these words, but they are the words of Jesus, who will judge all men and deeds. Jesus says this synagogue is not acting like real Jews are supposed to act. They lie. They are not real Jews. (Romans 9:6ff) Jesus reverses the words of Isaiah (45:14; 49:23; 60:14) that say Gentiles will bow down before Jews because they have the word of God, and are God's people. He says this disobedient synagogue will be in the Gentiles' place and the church (many of them Gentiles) will be in the place of the Jews, because they are the people of God.

> 10 Because you have kept the word of My perseverance, I also will keep you from the hour of testing, that hour which is about to come upon the whole world, to test those who dwell on the earth.

They have kept the word of Jesus that He perseveres for us. Because of that, Jesus kept them from the hour (a short time) of testing that came upon the "whole world." I do not, as others do, see this as a futuristic prophecy about the end of time. (Although if we keep His word He may do the same for us if any future time of testing should come.) I see this as a needed word of comfort for the Philadelphian Church, that the persecution coming to the other cities will not come to Philadelphia. The coming persecution the churches needed to be prepared for were local in nature. The local Asiarchs (or rulers of Asia), wanted to prove their loyalty to Rome by making everyone say "Caesar is Lord" and worshiping him. Jesus will not allow this to come to Philadelphia. He has shut the door on it.

I understand the "whole earth" in the Roman way of speaking. They believed their Empire to be the whole earth. (Luke 2:1)

The church here, again is in Smyrna, has had no condemnation from Jesus (Romans 8:1). It is nice that they were sinless, for there is no one without sin, but rather they were dealing with their sin and growing in grace so there was no need to point them out or condemn them for things they knew about and were working on. Like Job they were perfect, not because they never sinned but because their sin was covered by the cross of Christ. This proves that this is a divine book because people can always find fault, like Job's comforters—but Jesus, who knows the hearts of men, knows when His churches are doing a good job, and when they need correction.

11 I am coming quickly; hold fast what you have, in order that no one take your crown.

Jesus is coming quickly. It is the historic teaching of the Church that Jesus is soon to return. No one on earth nor the Angels in Heaven know when that day or hour is but it will be soon. Those who need to better repent. Those doing a good job need to hold fast what they have so that they do not lose their crown.

It has been for 2,000 years, and still is, the teaching of the Christian Church that Jesus is coming soon. Those in Philadelphia have no reason to fear as other churches do. They are ready. The only thing for them to do is keep up the good work. They need to hold fast these things.

That some one could take your crown, (stephonos—the crown you earn by winning a race) reminds me of Paul's warnings in Colossians 2 that no one "Takes you captive . . . (v.8), . . . acts as your judge . . . (v.16), "or . . . keeps defrauding you of your prize" (v.18).

12 He who overcomes, I will make him a pillar in the temple of My God, and he will not go out from it any more; and I will write upon the name of My God, and the name of the

City of My God, the new Jerusalem, which comes down out
of heaven from My God, and My new name.

In the Great Earthquake of A.D. 17 many in Philadelphia
ran out of town so that buildings would not fall on them
and began to make their homes outside the city. They went
out, but they never came back. Jewish believers were kicked
out of the Synagogue they grew up in because they found
the one who fulfilled the Old Testament. They were not
allowed to come back. He who overcomes will be made a
pillar in the Temple of God and no one can kick him out.

Those Jews who lied about what Moses said and what
God loves, will understand that God loves each one of these
in the church. Jesus will make them a pillar in the Temple
of God and no one can throw them out of it. Just as a Roman
or Greek temple needs pillars to stand and they even make
up the Temple, so in God's Temple His faithful people are
not only a part of it; they *are* the Church. They may get
thrown out of the synagogues in Philadelphia or Smyrna,
but never out of God's Temple.

The city of Philadelphia twice received a new name,
(although they did not keep them), when they received
money from Rome. To this city, receiving a new name is a
good thing, because it comes with blessings. The blessings
of Rome are temporary, and the new names did not last.
The blessings of God are eternal and His new names last
forever. To know the name of God is to know God.

13 He who has an ear, let him hear what the Spirit says to
the churches.

For whoever wishes to save his life shall lose it: and whoever loses his life for My sake and the gospel's shall save it.

—Mark 8:35

Now about that time Herod the king laid hands on some who belonged to the church, in order to mistreat them.

And he had James the brother of John put to death with a sword.

—Acts 12:1-2

Laodicea

14 And to the angel of the church in Laodicea write:

Forty-five miles southeast of Philadelphia is Laodicea, our last stop on our postal road. The city is the farthest east of all the seven churches and is located on the Lycus river near Colossae and Hierapolis. Laodicea is also the richest of all the cities. When the great earthquake hit all seven cities in A.D. 60 Laodicea rebuilt without asking for funds from Rome. The city boasted a great medical school famous for its ear and eye salve, and wool garments. Agricultural and commercial prosperity brought banking industry to the city. Laodicea had a large Jewish population but they did not attack the church here as they did in Smyrna and Philadelphia. Perhaps part of the problem of this church is that they were so tepid in their beliefs that they did not inspire opposition (Luke 6:24–25).

This church is the poor little rich church. Mentioned in Colossians 2:1 and 4:16, it was probably founded by Epaphras, and when Paul wrote to the Colossians, Archippus was probably the pastor. "In the year 361 a council was held here which established the New Testament Canon." (Linsky, p. 151)

The Amen, the Faithful and true Witness, the Beginning of the creation of God, says this: "The Amen" identifies himself with a word most people only know at the end of a prayer. It is a Hebrew word for "true," sometimes translated "so be it." In Isaiah 65:16 God identifies himself as the God of truth, with this same Hebrew word, "Amen." In the normal use of Amen you only use the word after something else is said and you know it to be the truth. You would never use the word to begin a sentence because you might make a mistake in what you are about to say. However, Jesus used the word before he said something He wanted His disciples to understand, and he used it twice. "Amen Amen, I say unto you . . . " This would usually be translated Truly Truly, or in King James, Verily, Verily. In Hebrew, using a word twice doubles it. Only Jesus would be bold enough to say Amen twice before He speaks, because He is truth.

"The Faithful and True Witness: " Jesus wants the readers to be faithful witnesses, as He was a faithful witness of the Father. He was faithful unto death.

"The Beginning of the creation of God": the one who began creation. These words would be familiar to the Laodicians who had read Colossians (1:15–17). It means that Jesus is the source of creation; He began it. It cannot mean (as the Arians falsely said) that Jesus is the first one created, because He is different from all the things created (v. 16). He is Eternal God.

15 I know your deeds, that you are neither cold nor hot; I would that you were cold or hot.

16 So because you are lukewarm, and neither hot nor cold, I will spit you out of My mouth.

Cold as in dead, frozen dead. Nominal Christians go to church and know that their lives are not right, yet they take solace in the fact that at least they go to church. They think in the final judgment that will help them. It would be better if they did not go at all, then they might know they need salvation. (Matthew 12:30, 1 John 2:15, James 4:4)

Hierapolis had Hot Springs, Colossae had cold water, Laodicea for all its wealth had to pipe water in and it was not as good. Mounce quotes Rudwick and Green when he says that "The contrast is between the hot medicinal waters of Hierapolis and the cold, pure waters of Colossae. Thus the church in Laodicea 'was providing neither refreshment for the spiritually weary, nor healing for the spiritually sick. It was totally ineffective, and thus distasteful to its Lord.' " (Mounce, p. 125)

Jesus does not say as the text here indicates that he will spit them out, but that he is about to. (Lenski, p. 155) There is time to repent. Prophecy is given so that people will repent.

17 Because you say, "I am rich, and have become wealthy, and have need of nothing," and you do not know that you are wretched and miserable and poor and blind and naked.

In the same way the Church was rich and bland. Too rich to ever need anything from God. They never knew how much they really did need. This is the Church we in America identify with more than any other. Rich and complacent we look to our own will and ways to salve things than rather rely on God. We are poor and naked, and miserable and blind.

18 I advise you to buy from Me gold refined by fire, that you may become rich, and white garments that you may clothe yourself and that the shame of your nakedness may not be revealed; and the eye salve to anoint your eyes, that you may see.

The Church in Laodicea would say; "Well, maybe we need some things—but we don't need gold, we have that; we don't need garments, or eye salve, we make those and get them wholesale."

Jesus says, 'You need My gold. While you are rich to men, you are not rich to me. But if the money is no good, how can one buy gold?" On the last day of the feast (John 7:37) Jesus stood and quoted Isaiah 55:1 where everyone is invited to buy without money (Revelation 22:17). By grace you receive the gold He has for you, but it is gold refined in fire. It won't cost you anything to receive it, but it will cost you dearly to keep it.

Now that you have gold you need to buy white garments, and not those black ones you have. God brings us from darkness to light. Could the reference to covering the "shame of their nakedness" mean that they could be found in the ritual pagan orgies?

Now that we have everyone clothed, we can fix their eyes. Like the Pharisees before them, this church, and many others today, are blind to their own sin. Jesus said "For judgment I came into this world, that those who do not see may see; and that those who see may become blind." (John 9:39, also see 9:41).

19 Those whom I love, I reprove and discipline; be zealous therefore, and repent.

If you are a child of God you can know it by the discipline that you have received. You might have noticed people who get by with sin and seem to get away it (Psalms 73). The reason is that they are not God's children. I do not discipline children that are not mine. God does not discipline children that are not His. His children He disciplines. Hebrews 12:3–13 teaches us that when troubles come it could be just hatred from the world or it could be discipline from the Lord and we should learn from it. What we should learn is to repent. (also see Proverbs 3:12) God loves us and forgives our sins—but that does not mean that there are not consequences to our actions. David was forgiven of his sin, yet did not die (2 Samuel 12), but the sword did not depart out of his house. Paul was forgiven for persecuting the church, yet God told Ananias, "I will show him how much he must suffer for My name's sake" (Acts 9:16). If you are not disciplined, you are not loved by God.

20 Behold, I stand at the door and knock; if any one hears My voice and opens the door, I will come in to him, and will dine with him, and he with Me.

The scariest thing said in this section is verse 20. A very familiar verse that we use evangelistically in sermons to reach the lost in our hearing, perhaps reminding them of the famous painting by Holman Hunt (*The Light of the World*) which portrays Jesus outside the door of our hearts knocking, with no latch on the outside; we must let Him in. What makes this so scary is that it is not for those outside the church—it is for those inside the church. Here is a church where Jesus is on the outside. I wonder how many churches are like that? There is not much hope of Jesus getting in because He is not wanted. However, if any individual in the church will open the door, Jesus will have dinner and fellowship with him. This is where revival starts with one person who prays, and gets right with God, and seeks to reach those in the church, till the whole church returns to the Lord, or the few get kicked out and start a real church.

21 He who overcomes, I will grant to him to sit down with Me on My throne, as I also overcame and sat down with My Father on His throne.

Overcoming is not easy. It means misunderstanding, confusion, lies, confiscation, persecution, tribulation, and death. With all of that we have the confidence that Jesus is with us (Matthew 28:20) and that He, Himself, went through all that we go through and more; and He overcame the world, the flesh, and the devil. If we overcome as He did, with His help of course, we get to sit on His throne. What more could could anyone ask for than to sit on the throne with Jesus?

22 He who has an ear, let him hear what the Spirit says to the churches.

But be on your guard; for they will deliver you up to the courts, and you will be flogged in the synagogues, and you will stand before governors and kings for My sake, as a testimony to them.

And the gospel must first be preached to all the nations.

And when they arrest you and deliver you up, do not be anxious beforehand about what you are to say, but say whatever is given you in that hour; for it is not you who speak, but it is the Holy Spirit.

—Mark 13:9–11

I know where you dwell, where Satan's throne is; and you hold fast My name, and did not deny My faith, even in the days of Antipas, My witness, My faithful one, who was killed among you, where Satan dwells.

—Revelation 2:13

4

The Throne

1 After these things I looked, and behold, a door standing open in heaven, and the first voice which I had heard, like the sound of a trumpet speaking with me, said, "Come up here, and I will show you what must take place after these things."

This verse has nothing to do with the rapture of the Church at all. This verse has to do with John going up to see the revelation. This is John's invitation to come up to heaven and see the revelation; but from Heaven you can see heaven and earth so that we will be going back and forth. Jesus was the one talking to him so, it is Jesus who asks him to come up.

2 Immediately I was in the spirit; and behold, a throne was standing in heaven, and One sitting on the throne.

John accepts the invitation and his spirit stands in Heaven. This time "in the spirit" could be understood in a different way in Chapter 1. In Chapter 1 it seems to describe his spiritual communion with God, where here it seems to be more literal, although it is not necessarily so. It could be that God came to John in his regular communion time. He is brought right to the throne room of God Himself.

3 And He who was sitting was like a jasper stone and a sardius in appearance; and there was a rainbow around the throne, like an emerald in appearance.

What does God look like? John describes God in terms of costly jewels. Precious, rare, expensive, exquisite; obviously John is not going to tell us what the Father looks like since he is Spirit, but we get the feeling of greatness on the throne. Just as one would wonder and be fascinated at a perfect diamond, there is wonder and beauty looking at God. Yet while His beauty is like that of a jasper stone, rather than reflect light He radiates light.

The rainbow could be a halo in translation. If you wondered where all the artists got halos for every saint, this is where. Yet I prefer rainbow. I like to think that God has a reminder of the Covenant with Noah right there. Even the rainbow reflects the Glory of God as costly gems.

4 And around the thrones were twenty-four thrones; and upon the thrones I saw twenty-four elders sitting, clothed in white garments, and golden crowns on their heads.

Twelve is the number of the people of God. There are twelve children of Israel; twelve tribes, twelve minor prophets, and twelve Apostles. Both the New and Old Covenants have 12 leaders for the people. The twenty-four elders are representative of the people of God in both covenants. Some argue that it could not be that way because John as an Apostle would be seeing himself. Well! First you are getting too literal. Second, you don't know that John did not see himself, although he had no time to meet them all individually. Third, someone could hold John's office for him till it was time for him to take his place. Fourth, in Hebrew thought if one was missing it would still be counted as twenty-four. Finally, I did not say these were the twelve Sons of Israel and the Twelve Apostles, I said they represent the people of God in the two Covenants.

They sit on thrones and they rule with Christ by his Grace. They are in white garments washed in the Blood of the Lamb. They are given golden crowns, for God has called them to rule.

> 5 And from the throne proceed flashes of lightning and sounds and peals of thunder. And there were seven lamps of fire burning before the throne, which are the seven spirits of God;

In our modern day we dismiss the thunder and lightning because we can explain the causes; yet in their presence we still jump or hide. God's throne is more dangerous than lightning and scarier than thunder.

The seven lamps are the seven spirits of God. Seven lamps adorn the Holy place of the Tabernacle. We usually associate them with candlesticks as in chapter 1, and the menorahs the Jews still use. Yet in the Tabernacle they were really lampstands that seven small lamps sat on. The olive oil in those lamps is symbolic of the Holy Spirit. I believe the seven spirits of God is a symbolic way of speaking of the Holy Spirit. Others see these as the seven archangels. Whichever interpretation you choose will not affect the overall interpretation of the book. There is no other representative symbol for the Holy Spirit in Chapter 4 if this is the archangels, and there is no other representative for the seven archangels (if there be seven archangels) if this is the Holy Spirit.

> 6 and before the throne there was, as it were, a sea of glass like crystal; and in the center and around the throne, four living creatures full of eyes in front and behind.

The sea separates John from the seven Churches while he is on Patmos. The Crystal Sea separates the throne from the Seven Churches. The Jews were not a sea-going people as the Phoenicians were. They saw the sea as an unstable place of chaos and death.

In close proximity of the Throne are the Four Living Ones. They are described here and in Isaiah, and in Ezekiel. The descriptions are not exact, but are close enough that we can understand that they are the same. The difference between Isaiah and Ezekiel is that in Ezekiel they had wheels. The Jews were in exile and away from the place where God met with them, so the Throne of God came equipped to come to them. Here the first thing we note about the Living Ones is that they are full of eyes. They see everything, they are very intelligent. God does not surround himself with dummies.

7 And the first creature was like a lion, and the second creature like a calf, and the third creature had a face like that of a man, and the fourth creature was like a flying eagle.

The Four Living Ones represent the four kinds of created life. The lion represents the wild land animals and insects that don't fly. The calf represents the domesticated land animals. The man of course represents human life. And the flying eagle represents the birds and fish and insects that fly. They are representative of life on earth. They are representative of creation.

8 And the Four Living Creatures, each one of them having six wings, are full of eyes around and within; and day and night they do not cease to say, "Holy, Holy, Holy is the Lord God, the Almighty who was and who is and who is to come."

Why did the Four Living Creatures continue to cry, "Holy, Holy, Holy?" Was that their job? Are they just to repeat the line like parrots? No, these are highly intelligent creatures; that's what is meant by "full of eyes." God does not surround Himself with dummies. They have, judging by their appearance, been in existence since creation. Isaiah saw them and so did Ezekiel. They have the best view, from the Throne of God, and they have seen everything. Their honest report (God would not surround Himself with those who are not honest) is that God is the Holiest. In Hebrew to speak in the superlative you say it three times. God is Holy, Holy, Holy. He is also the Almighty and Eternal God.

> 9 And when the living creatures give glory and honor and thanks to Him who sits on the throne, to Him who lives forever and ever,

> 10 the twenty-four elders will fall down before Him who sits on the throne, and worship Him who lives forever and ever, and will cast their crown before the throne, saying,

> 11 "Worthy art Thou, our Lord and our God, to receive the glory and honor and power; for Thou didst create all things, and because of Thy will they existed, and were created."

Worship of God is going on in Heaven. If you don't like to worship God on earth, why do you think you will like Heaven? Heaven is the place where proper praise of God will continue. Hell is the place for those who refuse to give God His praise. There are only these two places. Church is a place we go to, to learn how to worship God rightly so that we will be fit for Heaven. It takes a lifetime to get it. If you don't like to go to church, you won't like Heaven.

When the Four Living Ones do what is right and natural for them, worship God, then the twenty-four elders agree. They also love to worship God, and say what is true about Him. They throw their crowns at His feet, for He is Lord of all. They declare that God is worthy of glory. We are not familiar with this much worship because no one on earth is worthy of glory, honor, and power, but God is. They declare their three-fold doxology.

The twenty-four elders declare that God is worthy of praise if for no other reason than Creation. We exist by the will and the grace of God. God gives life and man has no business taking the life God gave. Man cannot create; only God can. Only God sustains life. Only for God does everything exist. Later we will find more to praise God for, but to begin is enough.

And you will be hated by all on account of My name, but it is the one who has endured to the end who will be saved.

—Mark 13:13

Then there was James, who was known as the brother of the Lord. . . . This James, whom the early Christians surnamed the Righteous because of his outstanding virtue, was the first as the records tell us, to be elected to the episcopal throne of the Jerusalem Church . . . was thrown down from the parapet and beaten to death with a fuller's club.

—Eusebius, *The History of the Church*, p. 72

5

The Lion

1 And I saw in the right hand of Him who sat on the throne a book written inside and on the back, sealed with seven seals.

Now that the stage is set, the action begins. Yet there is something new on the set. God is holding in His right hand (the place where Jesus stands) a book. The book is full of information. The pages are written on both sides. The book is important because it has seven seals. Do the seals all work together to seal up the book, or if you take off one seal can you read part of it? Many commentators bring up the fact that in Rome, wills looked like this scroll. Rolled up and sealed—and only the right people in the family could break the seal and read the will.

2 And I saw a strong angel proclaiming with a loud voice, "Who is worthy to open the book and to break the seals?"

What is important is that not just anyone can read what is written in this book. An important book in the Hand of God can only be read by someone who is worthy. A call goes out everywhere to find someone worthy to read the book.

3 And no one in heaven, or on the earth, or under the earth, was able to open the book, or to look into it.

The call goes all over Heaven, all over the earth, and under the earth. There are no other places to look. The one who can read the book now becomes more important than the book itself. No one living in Heaven and earth, or dead under the earth can read the book.

4 And I began to weep greatly, because no one was found worthy to open the book, or to look into it;

Now John has come all this way to hear the message of God, and there it is at God's right hand—but no one is worthy to take and read it. Not even John is worthy to read the book. He has no message for the seven Churches. He has come all this way, but God is too Holy and man is too sinful to receive the message. John gets caught up in this drama and begins to weep greatly for the great need to come between God and man.

5 and one of the elders said to me, "Stop weeping; behold, the Lion that is from the tribe of Judah, the Root of David, has overcome so as to open the book and the seven seals."

Now we can stop weeping, a champion is come. One who is strong and has overcome so as to open the book. One who is worthy is found and he is called the Lion of the Tribe of Judah. (Genesis 49:9 & 10) He is associated with the King of the beasts.

6 And I saw between the throne (with the four living creatures) and the elders a Lamb standing, as if slain, having seven horns and seven eyes, which are the seven spirits of God, sent out into all the earth.

Between God and his angels and man, the elders, dwells one who is both God and man. But what John sees is not a strong lion, but rather a lamb, not even a grown sheep but a lamb, and even worse than that the lamb is slain. Yet the lamb stands. He stands as if slain; I'm not sure what that means because if he was slain he would lie down.

John the Baptist saw Jesus pass by and said, "Behold the Lamb of God who takes away the sin of the world." (John 1:29) The Lamb slain is as much a fulfillment of what the Messiah would be as the Lion of the Tribe of Judah, the suffering servant of Isaiah 53 and the Almighty King of Psalm 2. This Lamb that was slain as the perfect Passover Lamb now stands (risen from the dead) and now has perfect power. He has seven horns (perfect power), and seven eyes, which we don't have to guess at: they are the Seven Spirits of God, which see what goes on on the earth. The Seven Spirits, or complete Spirit of God, was in Chapter 4 as Seven lamps now that light reflects in the Eyes of the Lamb.

7 And He came, and He took it out of the Right Hand of Him who sat on the throne.

Jesus takes the book or scroll from the Right Hand of God. That is the extent of the action in this chapter. The rest of the book reacts to this action.

8 And when He had taken the book, the four living creatures and the twenty-four elders fell down before the Lamb, having each one a harp, and golden bowls full of incense, which are the prayers of the saints.

Now the four living ones responded to this action by worshiping the Lamb. Worship must be for God alone, (Matt. 4:10; Deut. 6:13) and God will not share his Glory with another (Isaiah 42:8). Only God is worshipped. The Lamb is God.

The four living ones and the 24 elders fall down and worship, but do the living ones have harps or is it just the 24 elders? This is where we get the idea that everyone in heaven has a harp. The old joke about the fellow who said his wife was like an angel—always up in the air and harping—comes from this verse. The meaning is they are like David who was skillful with a harp and could make a song to celebrate everytime God worked in his life.

They also hold golden bowls full of incense. Brass bowls were used outside the Tabernacle. Inside the utensils were Gold (Exodus 25). Incense we are told symbolizes the prayers of the saints. A little incense goes a long way. In the 1960s when I was a youth, other youths used incense to cover up the smell of the pot they were smoking. A little incense can permeat a whole building. One of the questions the seven Churches wanted to have answered was: Does God hear our prayers? We pray about the situation down here and it doesn't look like anyone cares. God hears the prayers just as sure as anyone surrounded with 24 or 28 bowls of incense can smell it. God hears the prayers of the saints.

9 And they sang a new song, saying, "Worthy art Thou to take the book, and to break its seals; for Thou wast slain, and didst purchase for God with Thy blood men from every tribe and tongue and people and nation."

A new song always follows a new act of God. It is appropriate to respond to an act of God with song, and if you are so gifted, write a new song because God has done a new thing.

Yet the song is not about a new work of the Lamb taking up the scroll, but, rather, about the fact that He is worthy to take the scroll. The reason He is worthy is because he died on the cross for our sins. He was obedient to God even to death on the cross. And in that great act he fulfilled the law and the prophets and redeemed us from our sins. He paid the debt that our sin incurred. With His blood He paid for our sins and redeemed us so that we may again serve God. The Jewish Messiah saved not only Jews but people from all nations who trust in Him.

The center of prophecy is here, on the cross, not in our future but on what Jesus did for us on the cross.

10 And Thou hast made them to be a kingdom and priests to our God; and they will reign upon the earth.

Not only are our sins forgiven but we have a job to do. We are in the Kingdom of God, and we are priests (1 Peter 2:9) to the world. All believers are priests to God who stand before God and pray for those they know and work with and live around. The priesthood of the believer is more than just a doctrine: it is a commission. It is work we must do.

And they will reign on the earth. The way to reign is to serve. The way to rule is to learn obedience, as Jesus did. He was obedient unto death and rules the world. To rule with Him we must be obedient.

11 And I looked, and I heard the voice of many angels around the throne and the living creatures and the elders; and the number of them was myriads of myraids, and thousands of thousands.

A myriad is more than you can count. John did not live in a society where millions and billions of dollars are spent on a daily or annual basis. Once you get over multiple thousands you've lost most people (including me). More angels than you could count, surrounded the throne area.

12 saying with a loud voice, "Worthy is the Lamb that was slain to receive power and riches and wisdom and might and honor and glory and blessing."

The angels agree that Jesus is worthy not only to take the scroll but to receive 7 blessings. This is a seven-fold doxology. Worship continues to the intelligent created angels.

13 And every created thing which is in heaven and on the earth and under the earth and on the sea, and all the things in them, I heard saying, "To Him who sits on the throne, and to the Lamb, be blessing and honor and glory and dominion forever and ever."

All that is created will worship Him. Philippians 2:5–11 speaks of a future time when this will happen but in Heaven, where John sees the Revelation, Time is not a factor. All creation should and will worship. This worship is a four-fold doxology.

14 And the four living creatures kept saying, "Amen." And the elders fell down and worshipped.

The worship of the angels and every created thing prompts the four living ones to worship and agree, with an Amen, which means "so be it." And the elders are prompted to more worship.

For truly in this city there were gathered together against Thy holy servant Jesus, whom Thou didst anoint, both Herod and Pontius Pilate, along with the Gentiles and the peoples of Israel,

to do whatever Thy hand and Thy purpose predestined to occur.

And now, Lord, take note of their threats, and grant that Thy bond-servants may speak Thy word with all confidence,

—Acts 4:27–29

Peter was brought from thence (prison) for execution, when, after being severely scourged, he was crucified with his head downward; which position, however, was at his own request.

Paul . . . returning to Rome, he was again apprehended, and, by the order of Nero, martyred, by beheading.

About the same time Saints James, Philip, Matthew, Mark, Matthias, Jude, Bartholomew, Thomas, and Luke the Evangelist also suffered martyrdom for the cause of Christ.

—*Foxe's Book of Martyrs,* pp. 12–13

6

The Seals

1 And I saw when the Lamb broke one of the seven seals, and I heard one of the four living creatures saying as with a voice of thunder, "Come."

Chapter six begins in earnest the visions of the Book. Up till this point you could just interpret the text without taking a stand on any view; but at chapter 6 you must take a stand. Most commentators want to sell you on their view in the introduction, unlike Dr. Ray F. Robbins, in his book *The Revelation of Jesus Christ,* who never takes a stand until Chapter 6. I won't tell you the stand he takes—I'll let you find and read the book. I never like to give away the secret.

2 And I looked, and behold, a white horse, and he who sat on it had a bow; and a crown was given to him; and he went out conquering, and to conquer.

The opening of the first seal brings the first of the four horsemen of the apocalypse. The first horse is a white horse; its rider has a bow and a crown and he goes out to conquer. These things suggest that this is Jesus who will also later ride a white horse and conquer. There are problems with this view. The first is that Jesus is following a command given by one of the living ones. Second, Jesus here would be part of four and not standing on his own. Third, the other three are not that nice a group to hang with.

Well if it isn't Jesus and it looks like Jesus, maybe it's the Antichrist? This is another view and he would fit more with the other three horsemen. Would even the Antichrist want to be one of four? The word Antichrist never occurs in the Book of Revelation. I believe that the four horsemen represent one basic idea. That idea is War.

Rome prided its rule with the peace it provided. The Pax Romana, the peace of Rome, was characterized of the empire. It was what allowed Paul to carry the gospel to Rome. Rome guarded its peace with brute force. The judgment that would fall on the empire is that war would undo it.

War always begins with a sting of propaganda. The king, or politician, comes to the people and paints a picture of a righteous call or great reward and it is sold to those who would have to fight or pay or both. It is sold as a righteous thing, something as pure as the Messiah himself. It is sold as a rider on a white horse with a bow and crown. Not as a regular foot soldier who has to slug his way through the mud.

Dr. Ray Summers sees in the first horseman a Parthian soldier. That may be because the Romans lost two battles to those just east of the Seven Churches. I believe that it is more important to notice not that He is Parthian, but that he is not Roman. The Romans have done their conquering and now it is someone else's turn.

3 And when He broke the second seal, I heard the second living creature saying, "Come."

4 And another, a red horse, went out; and to him who sat on it, it was granted to take peace from the earth, and that man should slay one another; and a great sword was given to him.

The second stage of war is to actually begin to take peace from the earth. It is given by God for this one to succeed. Peace is not an absence of war but a state of living with others. To make war work you must take that away from the people. Slaying one another is not all there is to war; it is just the second stage. The rider of the red horse is given by God a great sword.

5 And when He broke the third seal, I heard the third living creature saying, "Come." And I looked, and behold, a black horse; and he who sat on it had a pair of scales in his hand.

6 And I heard as it were a voice in the center of the four living creatures saying, "A quart of wheat for a denarius, and three quarts of barley for a denarius; and do not harm the oil and the wine."

Famine follows battle. Wars are fought many times on farm fields. Crops that are not carried to the front to feed the troops are destroyed by war, or stolen by the soldiers who usually are farmers. If they are fighting they are not farming. Therefore not enough food is produced for normal consumption. A denarius is what a man makes in one day. A quart of wheat is what a man consumes in one day.

Barley is not as good a grain as wheat but if a man is married he can better feed his family. If you spend all your money on wheat you cannot afford the oil or wine whether it is harmed or not.

7 And when he broke the fourth seal, I heard the voice of the fourth living creature say "Come."

8 And I looked, and behold, an ashen horse; and he who sat on it had the name Death; and Hades was following with him. And authority was given to them over a fourth of the earth, to kill with sword and with famine and with pestilence and by the wild beasts of the earth.

The last horse is death and Hades was following, whether on another horse, or on the same horse, or walking, running, or flying by the side of the 4th horse. War in the end has taken its toll and in the balance is death. War is Hell. War rides again and again on these horses and the last one is death. Wars are sometimes necessary but they are never good. In only a few cases is the cause ever really noble or just. It never is the great cause the first horseman says it is. At best it is an ugly job that must be done. At worst it is a disaster that should never have been done and you find yourself fighting on the wrong side (always a possibility; See Chapter 8, The Red Horse and its Rider, in Billy Graham's book *Approaching Hoofbeats/The Four Horsemen of the Apocalypse*).

While Rome thought of itself as the whole earth, they also knew there was more of a world outside their empire. They would also speak of having $1/4$th of the Earth. God says because you have declared war on my people I will declare war on the Roman Empire.

9 And when He broke the fifth seal, I saw underneath the altar the souls of those who had been slain because of the word of God, and because of the testimony which they had maintained;

Now we come to the heart of the book; this is what the readers want to know about. In one of the churches there had already been at least one death that we know of. From the stoning of Stephen to John's writing this letter, many had lost their lives for the sake of the gospel, including 11 of the twelve, Paul, James and many more. They had been found guilty only of the Word of God and the Testimony of Jesus. All Christians should be so guilty. These believers seem to be hiding under the altar, but that it not quite right.

We can't see this picture because we don't see sacrifice as a part of our worship. When an animal was sacrificed its blood was poured out at the side of the altar. The blood would run under the altar, and the life of the flesh is in the blood. The life of the believers is poured out as a sacrifice to God which pleases him. Their death does not please God but their faithfulness does. They maintained the testimony, even in the face of torture and death. In the face of so much luxury and selfishness in the Roman world there came a group of people who loved something more than their freedom, privilege, position, comfort, happiness, family, friends, government, and even life itself.

We live in society which is greatly influenced by the Humanist philosophy, which believes that human life is the most important good and the worst thing that can happen is that you die. This is not true in Christianity where the worst thing that can happen is that we sin. Sin separates us from God, and keeps us from the victory Jesus wants us to have.

> 10 and they cried out with a loud voice, saying, "How long, O Lord, holy and true, wilt Thou refrain from judging and avenging our blood on those who dwelt on the earth?"

The saints are not just part of the furniture, they begin not just to speak but to ask an important question. Don't you have some question you want to ask when you get to Heaven? The question they ask has led some who live in the safety of Western, 20th Century Christianity, to say that the question and therefore The Book of Revelation is sub-Christian. According to this view, Christians are to take the hardships without speaking out (1 Corinthians 11:24–30). Well they did while on earth, and now in Heaven they ask the question.

First of all they are not asking for personal vengeance, but they are asking for vindication. They proclaimed Jesus as God and refused to worship anyone or anything else. The Roman government had them killed to prove to the world that Rome is right through Roman might. Rome believes itself invincible, and the God of the Christians powerless to stop them. These believers do not care for vengeance but for the Kingdom of God. They laid down their lives and fully expected God to answer from Heaven with Judgment to prove that Jesus is more powerful than Caesar, and that they were not wrong or foolish to follow him. If God does not do something all Christians will be killed and Rome will win the day.

Second, they are not calling for anything that is not already in Scripture. God had said all through the Bible that he would judge the wicked as well as reward the righteous. Paul told us not to take vengeance but to leave it to God. When? It is a given in all Scripture that judgment will come; it is never stated anywhere that it will *not* come. The only question is not will it come, but WHEN?

The word saint means believer, literally translated "holy ones." What that means is that they were made holy through the blood of Christ. They were average believers who were tested to the limit of their faith and won by being faithful. The Catholic Church has made saints a special category of believers for the purpose of remembering the tribulation saints. Yet I doubt that they would say they were all that special. We need to remember the great thing that they did, however, we need not make them more than sinners redeemed through grace. We never know but that we might be called on to make that same choice. I pray that never happens, but as long as we must confront a sinful world that is a possibility. We should not seek martyrdom but we should never shrink from it.

Finally, the question they ask is the same one that the readers of Revelation are asking. Why does God allow this evil in the world? When is God going to do something about it?

> 11 And there was given to each of them a white robe; and they were told they should rest for a little while longer, until the number of their fellow servants and their brethren who were to be killed even as they had been, should be completed also.

Before we answer the question each of them receives a white robe. It reminds us of Joseph's colorful coat or the robes of the priests but it has a more important purpose. The last time the first readers of this Book saw the believers who died on the crosses, they were stripped of the clothes. The humiliation Rome inflicted on the believers is still on the mind of the churches. Those taken to the arenas to be killed by wild animals had their clothes torn and bloodied. They are given a white robe and their dignity.

Now John would like to say "it's all over! Boy, that was bad but now it's all over." But the truth is that it is not over. More believers must suffer, more believers must die. It is only A.D. 90; the persecution of the early church will continue until the Edict of Milan in 311. There is much more to come. All peace with the world is only temporary. If we faithfully speak for God we will incur the wrath of the world. To the saints under the altar the answer is to wait until all of this number is complete. We are not told what that number is; but when the number was complete the world knew that the saints were right to stand for Jesus, and Rome was wrong. That's what the saints wanted, for their death to count.

> 12 And I looked when He broke the sixth seal, and there was a great earthquake; and the sun became black as sackcloth made of hair, and the whole moon became like blood;

13 and the stars of the sky fell to the earth, as a fig tree casts its unripe figs when shaken by a great wind.

14 And the sky was split apart like a great scroll when it is rolled up; and every mountain and island were moved out of their places.

These visions do not come in chronological order, rather in emotional order. After seeing the saints who suffered we see a glimpse of the final Judgment that will right the wrong suffered by the saints. If you see stars in the sky, as it has been since the beginning of creation, then the world has not been judged . . . But it will! (Isaiah 34:1–17; Jeremiah 4:23–26)

15 And the kings of the earth and the great men and the commanders and the rich and the strong and every slave and free man, hid themselves in the caves and among the rocks of the mountains;

16 and they said to the mountains and to the rock, "Fall on us and hide us from the presence of Him who sits on the throne, and from the wrath of the Lamb;

17 for the great day of their wrath has come; and who is able to stand?"

When Jesus comes to judge the world and those who persecute His church, there will be no place to hide for kings or slaves or anyone. To be afraid of a Lamb is really something. Not a lion or a bear, not even a sheep or a ram, but a lamb! But this Lamb is the most powerful person ever. This Lamb is God. Caesar is not God. He is not even a god. He is a man in a lot of trouble.

"If the world hates you, you know that it has hated Me before it hated you.

"If you were of the world, the world would love its own; but because you are not of the world, but I chose you out of the world, therefore the world hates you."

—John 15:18–19

The governor pressed him further: "Swear, and I will set you free: execrate Christ." "For eighty-six years," replied Polycarp, "I have been His servant, and He has never done me wrong: how can I blaspheme my King who saved me?"

... "I'll have you destroyed by fire, unless you change your attitude!" Polycarp answered: "The fire you threaten burns for a time and is soon extinguished: there is a fire you know nothing about—the fire of the judgment to come and of eternal punishment, the fire reserved for the ungodly. But why do you hesitate? Do what you want."

... When he has offered up the Amen and completed his prayer, the men in charge lit the fire, and a great flame shot up.

—Eusebius, *The Martyrdom of Polycarp*, pp. 172–173

7

The People of God

1 After this I saw four angels standing at the four corners of the earth, holding back the four winds of the earth, so that no wind should blow on the earth or on the sea or on any tree.

Yes, God is going to judge the earth. But wait! Before we judge the earth we have much to do! Stop everything! Stop the four winds! The winds that come from the north, the south, the east, and the west. (Ezekiel 7:2)

2 And I saw another angel ascending from the rising of the sun, having the seal of the living God; and he cried out with a loud voice to the four angels to whom it was granted to harm the earth and the sea,

3 saying, "Do not harm the earth or the sea or the trees, until we have sealed the bond-servants of our God on their foreheads."

This idea parallels Ezekiel 9 where God judges all except those who "sigh and groan over all the abominations which are being committed in its midst." (v.4) And God has his angel mark them on the forehead. In Revelation everyone gets a mark; it is either the mark of God, or the mark of the Beast. The question is not do you have a mark; the question is which mark is it.

4 And I heard the number of those who were sealed, one hundred and forty-four thousand sealed from every tribe of the sons of Israel:

Who are the hundred and forty-four thousand? The Jehovah's Witnesses used to say that they were the 144,000 until they got more members than 144,000 and so they said only select, really special members get to go to Heaven and be a part of the 144,000 because that's all the room there is in Heaven; after that, Heaven is all full up. I had one of their followers try to tell me with a sincere heart that Earth is bigger than Heaven. So much for comic relief, now back to the Bible. The 144,000 are Jews, sons of Israel.

In Matthew 24 Jesus began to tell the disciples what their future would be after he left. It was a time they would live to see (v.34). In A.D. 66, the temple begun by Herod the Great was finally finished. This caused the Jews to decided they no longer needed the help of Rome, and they began a rebellion by defeating the small number of Roman troops in Israel. Rome sent more troops. By A.D. 70 Jerusalem and the temple were destroyed. By A.D. 74, another project of Herod the Great, the last holdout of the radical zealots, fell. These are the same radicals that were in the city of Jerusalem doing things to the citizens that were worse than the Romans would do. This is why Jesus warned his disciples when the time came to run to the hills and not the city (Matt. 24:15–22).

When you read Acts you discover that there was little love lost between the Jews who were Christians and the ones that were not. After the Romans destroyed Jerusalem, the Jews who were not Christians now had a new charge and reason to hate the Jews who were Christians. They called them traitors, because they left Jerusalem in its time of need. When it was pointed out that Jesus already told us it was a lost cause, and that his prophecy came true, the answer came back, "You made that up after the fact!" Not true; Luke records the same prophecy (Luke 17:31) and Luke was written before Acts, and Acts was written before Paul's death in A.D. 64 (Luke 1:1–4; Acts 1:1–3; 28:30–31). Yet the Jews were not convinced, and began a teaching that in A.D. 90 was passed in one of their councils that taught: If a Jew becomes a Christian he is no longer a Jew. Therefore, if a Jew becomes an atheist, agnostic, existentialist, communist, or right wing Republican then he is still Jewish. But if he becomes a Christian, his family will have a funeral for him, for to them he no longer exists. The message to the Church was, you will no longer get Jewish converts.

To this John has an answer from Jesus:

5 from the tribe of Judah, twelve thousand were sealed, from the tribe of Reuben twelve thousand were sealed, from the tribe of Gad twelve thousand,

6 from the tribe of Asher twelve thousand, from the tribe of Naphtali twelve thousand, from the tribe of Manasseh twelve thousand,

7 from the tribe of Simeon twelve thousand, from the tribe of Levi twelve thousand, from the tribe of Issachar twelve thousand,

8 from the tribe of Zebulun twelve thousand, from the tribe of Joseph twelve thousand, from the tribe of Benjamin, twelve thousand were sealed.

The numbers were symbolic; 12 is the people of God. Multiplying by 1,000 is used to magnify the other numbers. At least 12,000 believers from each tribe will become Christians. And so Jewish believers (in the beginning that's all there were) have been in church with us Gentiles for 2,000 years. Throughout the history of the Church, Jews have read Moses or Psalm 22, or Isaiah 53, and realized that Jesus was the promised Messiah. They then became complete as Jews.

The list is not complete. Dan is missing. Dan was that tribe that lived so far north that when King Jeroboam set up the two golden calves, he put one in Bethel near Jerusalem, (that one received condemnation as soon as he put it up) and the other one he put in Dan, so far north that they had forgotten they were the people of God and became just like all the other nations around them. If you want to totally get away from God, He will let you go. Yet to replace Dan there is listed Joseph, Manassah, and Levi. Levi and Joseph are two of the twelve sons of Israel. Joseph received the blessing of first-born so his two sons had a place as sons; that would make 13. But when it came time to divide the land, Levi as the priestly tribe did not get an allocation of land so there are only 12 tribes of Israel. Just as in the New Testament there were the 12 apostles, Judas hung himself, and he was replaced by another. 12 is the number of the people of God.

> 9 After these things I looked and behold, a great multitude, which no one could count, from every nation and all tribes and peoples and tongues, standing before the throne and before the Lamb, clothed in white robes, and palm branches were in their hands;

Now there is a different group. The Church began 100 percent Jewish, but it did not stay that way. The Good News has spread to every nation, tribe, people, and tongue, as the Old Testament said it would. They, like the saints under the altar, were in white robes and for the same reason. Yet their worship is Jewish. We Gentiles had to learn worship from our elder Jewish brothers.

94

10 and they cried out with a loud voice, saying, "Salvation to our God who sits on the throne, and to the Lamb."

The worship of the nations goes to God and to the Lamb. For it is the Lamb who brought salvation to us and brought us to God.

11 And all the angels were standing around the throne and around the elders and the four living creatures; and they fell on their faces before the throne and they worshipped God,

The elders and the living ones never miss an opportunity to worship God because, a. they love to do it, and b. it is right to do. I one time visited a Presbyterian church and the preacher was saying good things that needed an Amen. So being the uncouth Baptist I am I said it, although not too loud. But I was the only one. In Heaven we get to join in on the worship.

12 saying, "Amen, blessing and glory and wisdom and thanksgiving and honor and power and might, be to our God forever and ever. Amen.

Their Amen is followed by a seven-fold Doxology. Obviously they are not Presbyterian. Now you know I'm kidding my Calvinistic friends, but, seriously—in many churches today the congregation is treated more like an audience than people who have come to worship. Music is done for the congregation, by the choir or worship leaders. The congregation becomes a distant spectator of worship and not a participant.

13 And one of the elders answered, saying to me, "Those who are clothed in the white robes, who are they and from where have they come?"

14 And I said to him, "My Lord, you know." And he said to me, "These are the ones who come out of the great tribulation, and they have washed their robes and made them white in the blood of the Lamb.

My favorite hymn when preaching on the Book of Revelation is "I Know Whom I Have Believed" (337 in your *Baptist Hymnals*). The Chorus is from 2 Timothy 1:12. The verses say: I don't know; how Grace works, how faith works, how the Spirit moves, or when the Lord is going to come back. When you don't know something, say so. If you keep talking when you don't know, everyone will find out anyway.

They come from the great tribulation. Is this the same one that Jesus talked about in Matthew 24:21? No, Jesus talked about a great tribulation. There are many great tribulations! In the twentieth century we have had: World Wars I & II; the atomic bomb; Korea; Vietnam; Stalin's slaughter of the Ukraine (not to mention all those around him); the Turks' slaughter of the Armenians; Hitler's slaughter of the Jews; Pol Pot's slaughter of the Cambodians . . . All these are Great Tribulations. It would be silly to go to the victims of any of these and say, "Well you can thank your lucky stars you're not in the Great Tribulation!" That's silly talk. The Great Tribulation is emotional talk. When Jesus said it, it was a warning of something coming soon. When the elder here says it from the safety of Heaven I believe he was talking about earth and the Great Tribulation currently under way in A.D. 90. From up there it seems like there is always one going on down here.

Because this is a great multitude they are the ones throughout church history who witnessed unto death. This would even include those who died for the faith when an official tribulation was not taking place.

They have washed their dirty blood-stained robes in the blood of the Lamb and they come out white and not red.

96

15 "For this reason, they are before the throne of God; and they serve Him day and night in His temple; and He who sits on the throne shall spread His tabernacle over them.

Nothing can separate them from the love of God (Romans 8:35ff). They are before the Throne, in the Temple, covered with God's own Tabernacle. They are with God. Don't feel sorry for those that the Romans have killed for the faith. If I may be so bold, God has got them in a Holy Hug.

16 "They shall hunger no more, neither thirst anymore; neither shall the sun beat down on them, nor any heat;

The concern of the Seven Churches is the fate of those who died for the faith, and those who will soon face death. The believers watch fellow believers hang on crosses for days with the sun beating down on them. They are hungry, thirsty, and exposed to the burning sun with no clothes they are sunburned. This is the last image many believers have of the saints who have gone on, but they are not that way anymore. They have overcome and are now with God.

17 for the Lamb in the center of the throne shall be their shepherd, and shall guide them to springs of the water of life; and God shall wipe every tear from their eyes."

The Lamb is in the center of the throne. Jesus is one with God. (John 1:1)

The Lamb shall be the Shepherd. Yes, he is the Good Shepherd (John 10:7–18; Matthew 2:6; Psalm 23).

There is no longer any reason to pity them. They overcame, what will you do. You saw their tears, but now they are alright.

Remember the word that I said to you, "A slave is not greater than his master." If they persecuted Me, they will also persecute you; if they kept My word, they will keep yours also.

But all these things they will do to you for My name's sake, because they do not know the One who sent Me.

—John 15:20–21

Julian, a native of Cilicia, as we are informed by St. Chrysostom, was seized for being a Christian. He was tortured, but remained inflexible.

When all endeavours to make him recant his religion were found ineffectual, he was brought before a judge and whipped. He was then put into a leather bag, with a number of serpents and scorpions, and in that condition thrown into the sea.

—*Foxe's Book of Martyrs* pp. 21–22

8

The Trumpets

1 And when He broke the seventh seal, there was a silence in Heaven for about half an hour.

This is a dramatic pause, anticipating what will come next. This is not, as some have said, proof that there are no women in Heaven.

2 And I saw the seven angels who stand before God; and seven trumpets were given to them.

Wait a minute—what happened to the book, the scroll? We took off all the seals. We are not going to read it? What happened to the book? Some would say the rest of the vision is the book. Or maybe the book is no longer important. Just as in a dream the focus changes quickly, so the book drops from importance.

Now we have another set of seven. This time seven angels blowing trumpets.

3 And another angel came and stood at the altar, holding a golden censer; and much incense was given to him, that he might add it to the prayers of all the saints upon the golden altar which was before the throne.

4 And the smoke of the incense, with the prayers of the saints, went up before God out of the angel's hand.

5 And the angel took the censer; and he filled it with the fire of the altar and he threw it to the earth; and there followed peals of thunder and sounds and flashes of lightning and an earthquake.

6 And the seven angels who had the seven trumpets prepared themselves to sound them.

Now, what is going on? The angel begins to take the incense off the altar, and we don't have to guess what the incense symbolizes; we are told plainly, it is the prayers of the saints. God is working out His plans and His plans do not match the prayers of the saints. I see God saying to His people, what if I did what you ask me to do in your prayers. Let's play a "what-if" game; for the next two chapters God is going to give the people what they ask in their prayers. Then at the end of Chapter 9 we will analyze whether or not it was a good idea. Remember, we start with the prayers of the saints.

7 And the first sounded, and there came hail and fire, mixed with blood, and they were thrown to the earth; and a third of the earth was burned up, and a third of the trees were burned up, and all the green grass was burned up.

How dare these people attack the people of God! Do they not realize that God can send fire from Heaven as He did with Elijah? (II Kings 1; Luke 9:51–56)

8 And the second angel sounded, and something like a great mountain burning with fire was thrown into the sea; and a third of the sea became blood;

9 and a third of the creatures which were in the sea and had life, died; and a third of the ships were destroyed.

Rome rules not only land but also the sea. But they are not the Sovereign of the land and sea; the God of the Saints is. He could destroy their navy if he wanted.

10 And the third angel sounded, and a great star fell from Heaven, buring like a torch, and it fell on a third of the rivers and on the springs of waters;

11 and the name of the star is called Wormwood; and a third of the waters became wormwood; and many men died from the waters, because they were made bitter.

Why stop with the salt water when we could also destroy the fresh water as well?

12 And the fourth angel sounded, and a third of the sun and a third of the moon and a third of the stars were smitten, so that a third of them might be darkened and the day might not shine for a third of it, and the night in the same way.

This would show them who is boss. Mess with the sky and we'll show them who they're dealing with.

13 And I looked, and I heard an eagle flying in midheaven, saying with a loud voice, "Woe, woe, woe, to those who dwell on the earth, because of the remaining blasts of the trumpet of the three angels who are about to sound!"

"You ain't seen nothing yet!" Wait till you see what the saints have been praying for in Chapter 9. If you think this is too hard, imagine if it was your church family, or even your family members that the Government decided to persecute for following Jesus.

These things I have spoken to you, that you may be kept from stumbling.

They will make you outcasts from the synagogue; but an hour is coming for everyone who kills you to think that he is offering service to God.

—John 16:1–2

Lucian, a man of the highest character, self-disciplined and steeped in divinity, a presbyter of the Antioch diocese, was taken to Nicomedia, where the emperior (Maximin) then happened to be staying. Before the ruler he put forward his defence of the doctrine he upheld, and was sent to prison and to death.

—Eusebius 8:6.2, p. 362

9

The Locusts

1 And the fifth angel sounded, and I saw a star from heaven which had fallen to the earth; and the key of the bottomless pit was given to him.

If you want to torment the people on earth let's go get the best in the field. I mean this is a guy who really likes to do this bad stuff. Jesus said that he saw Satan fall from Heaven like lightning (Luke 10:18). Jesus did not say when that was. Nor are we sure that this angel that is opening the bottomless pit is Satan or just that he is going to let Satan and his goons out. If you want judgment, this is the one God uses to do it. In Chapter 8 we saw Judgments you could think of; in Chapter 9 God comes up with Judgments that the saints want that they could not even imagine.

2 And he opened the bottomless pit; and smoke went up out of the pit, like the smoke of a great furnace; and the sun and the air were darkened by the smoke of the pit.

3 And out of the smoke came forth locuts upon the earth; and power was given them, as the scorpions of earth have power.

4 And they were told that they should not hurt the grass of the earth, nor any green thing, nor any tree, but only the men that do not have the seal of God on their foreheads.

I'm not wanting to be an authority of the pit, because by the Grace of God I'm not going there. But it does have so much smoke coming out it blocks out the sun. The demon-locust set out on the earth but not as regular locust to harm the vegetation; that was done after the first angel sounded his trumpet. This time it's to torment the men of earth who do not carry the mark of God.

Now you say, if this reflexes the prayers of Christians then they should not pray this way. Perhaps not—but have you prayed that way? Would you like God to play the tape back when that guy cut you off on the freeway, or after the last deacons' meeting? We don't go through the things these saints went through.

5 And they were not permitted to kill anyone, but to torment for five months, and their torment was like the torment of a scorpion when it stings a man.

6 And in those days men will seek death and will not find it; and they will long to die and death flees from them.

7 And the appearance of the locust was like horses prepared for battle; and on their heads, as it were, crowns like gold, and their faces were like the faces of men.

8 And they had hair like the hair of women, and their teeth were like the teeth of lions.

9 And they had breastplates like breastplates of iron; and the sound of their wings was like the sound of chariots, of many horses rushing to battle.

10 And they have tails like scorpions, and stings; and in their tails is the power to hurt men for five months.

Please don't make any more of these things than what they are. They are instruments of torment and they are supposed to look as wicked as they are.

11 They have as king over them, the angel of the abyss; his name in Hebrew is Abaddon, and in Greek he has the name Apollyon.

The king over this is destruction, whether in Greek or Hebrew. Satan's goal is to destroy mankind. When people die they cannot repent and be saved.

12 The first woe is past; behold two more woes are still coming after these things.

13 And the sixth angel sounded, and I heard a voice from the four horns of the golden altar which is before God,

14 one saying to the sixth angel who had the trumpet, "Release the four angels that are bound at the great river Euphrates."

15 And the four angels, who had been prepared for the hour and day and month and year, were released, so that they might kill a third of mankind.

16 And the armies of the horsemen was two hundred million; I heard the number of them.

Rome could not conquer the armies of the east, as a matter of fact for the next thousand years armies would come from the east and attack the empire.

17 And this is how I saw in the vision the horses and those who sat on them: the riders had breastplates the color of fire

and of hyacinth and of brimstone; and the heads of the horses are like the heads of lions; and out of their mouths proceed fire and smoke and brimstone.

18 A third of mankind was killed by these three plagues, by the fire and the smoke and the brimstone, which proceeded out of their mouths.

19 For the power of the horse is in their mouths and in their tails; for their tails are like serpents and have heads; and with them they do harm.

If it is not bad enough to make these tribes of the east thirsty for Rome, we can put them on war horses like you have never seen before.

If the prayers of the saints came true that's what would happen. But by the Grace of God He does not do what we want but what He wants. Jesus prayed, "not my will but Thy will be done." No matter what we feel, we still want God's will to be done.

20 And the rest of mankind, who were not killed by these plagues, did not repent of the works of their hands, so as not to worship demons, and the idols of gold and of silver and of brass and of stone and of wood, which can neither see nor hear nor walk;

21 and they did not repent of their murders nor of their sorceries nor of their immortality nor of their thefts.

The main reason that God does not do it the way the saints have been praying is that it won't work. In the face of all the Judgments we could pray up, rebellious man would not repent and find Jesus as his Savior. They do not repent of their idol worship. They do not repent of killing believers for being believers. They do not repent of their drug dealing and occultic practices. They do not repent of their sexual deviance. They do not repent of taking the property of saints they have killed, and Church buildings they have stolen.

What will cause them to repent? They need to see Christianity lived out. We need saints to be faithful even unto death. The goal was never world conquest or domination; the goal is winning the world to faith in Christ.

But we have this treasure in earthen vessels, that the surpassing greatness of the power may be of God and not from ourselves;

we are afflicted in every way, but not crushed; perplexed, but not despairing;

persecuted, but not forsaken; struck down, but not destroyed;

always carrying about in the body the dying of Jesus, that the life of Jesus also may be manifested in our body.

—2 Corinthians 4:7–10

The great Council of Constance was approaching, and the confusion in Bohemia was certain to demand its consideration. (Jan) Hus was asked to present himself before it, and promised a "safe-conduct," afterward received, by the Holy Roman Emperor, Sigismund. Hus, though he felt his life in grave peril, determined to go, partly believing it his duty to bear witness to what he deemed the truth, and partly convinced that he could bring the council to his way of thinking. Shortly after his arrival in Constance he was imprisoned . . . He would not submit his conscience to the overruling judgment of the council . . . he was condemned and burned, meeting his death with the most steadfast courage.

—July 6, 1415, *A History of the Christian Church*
—By Williston Walker, pp. 272–273

10

The Little Book

1 And I saw another strong angel coming down out of heaven, clothed with a cloud; and the rainbow was upon his head, and his face was like the sun, and his feet like pillars of fire;

2 and he had in his hand a little book which was open. And he placed his right foot on the sea and his left on the land,

3 and he cried out with a loud voice, as when a lion roars; and when he had cried out, the seven peals of thunder uttered their voices.

4 And when the seven peals of thunder had spoken, I was about to write; and I heard a voice from heaven saying, "Seal up the things which the seven peals of thunder have spoken, and do not write them.

This is a great angel, and not Jesus. Jesus is never an angel and an angel is never Jesus. Now what is important in these four verses is that we do not know, cannot know what the seven peals of thunder said. We can only know what is revealed. Because John did not tell us what the seven thunders said, we cannot know. If you find someone who tries to unlock this mystery, understand that he does not know what he is talking about. My mother had a friend who she said knew who was buried in the Tomb of the Unknown Soldier in Washington, DC. When I asked her who it was she said she knew but she forgot right now. She probably also knows what the seven Thunders said.

He also has a book. Is this a different book than the one with the seals on it? I believe so, but we are not told.

> 5 And the angel whom I saw standing on the sea and on the land lifted up his right hand to Heaven.

> 6 and swore by Him who lives forever and ever, who created heaven and the things in it, and the earth and the things in it, and the sea and the things in it, that there shall be delay no longer,

The King James Version says at the end of v. 6 . . . Time shall be no longer. The NASB says: there shall be delay no longer. That is what it means, time is up. To say that there will be no more time is a philosophical problem that we do not need to address because that is not what the text says. God will not delay to judge the world and do what needs to be done. God is not asleep at the wheel. Things are moving along on time.

> 7 but in the days of the voice of the seventh angel, when he is about to sound, then the mystery of God is finished, as He preached to His servants and prophets.

The end will come on time. When the seventh angel sounds it will be the end of the world just as the prophets in the Old Testament, and the Apostles in the New Testament have said. Jesus has not delayed his coming or the consummation of the world. It is all moving on time.

> 8 And the voice which I heard from Heaven, I heard again speaking with me, and saying, "Go, take the book which is

open in the hand of the angel who stands on the sea and the land."

9 And I went to the angel, telling him to give me the little book. And he said to me, "Take it, and eat it; and it will make your stomach bitter, but in your mouth it will be sweet as honey."

10 And I took the little book out of the angel's hand and ate it, and it was in my mouth sweet as honey; and when I had eaten it my stomach was made bitter.

John is to eat, not read, this book (Jer. 15:16; Ezek. 2:8–3:3). It tastes great, but like a lot of food that is unfamiliar, it comes back to hurt you, in your stomach. This is the way of preaching Judgment. It feels good at first because the evil people who have done so much damage to so many other people, they deserve the judgment they get. Yet when you reflect on it later, with the heart of God, you realize that they sinned just as you sinned, and you deserve what they got. By the Grace of God you have been saved, they could have been saved. God does not take pleasure in Judgment (Ezek. 18:23). If your heart follows God you will also be sad. Sin makes us sick.

11 And they said to me, "You must prophesy again concerning many peoples and nations and tongues and kings."

But whether it makes us sick or not, we must preach, or prophesy. We must speak forth the word of God even if it upsets us. Justice must be and will be served. We must preach as John had to preach to everyone we can that the Judgment is coming, now is the time to repent.

Who shall separate us from the love of Christ? Shall tribulation, or distress, or persecution, or famine, or nakedness, or peril, or sword?

Just as it is written, "For Thy sake we are being put to death all day long; We are considered as sheep to be slaughtered."

But in all these things we overwhelmingly conquer through Him who loved us.

—Romans 8:35–37

Sir John Oldcastle of Herefordshire, also known as Lord Cobham, was a Lollard who tried to foment a rebellion after he had been accused as a heretic. His efforts ended in capture and execution. "And soon after," says a contemporary account of his followers, "there were drawn and hanged 36 upon one day, upon new gallows made for them upon the highway."

—1417 *The Church: From Pentecost to the Present* pp. 135–136

11

The Two Witnesses

1 And there was given me a measuring rod like a staff; and someone said, "Rise and measure the temple of God, and the altar, and those who worship in it."

When Nebuchadnezzar destroyed Solomon's Temple the Jews were devastated. Why did God allow the Gentiles to destroy His house? If they would have listened to the prophets they would know. God called on Ezekiel (Ezek. 40ff) to follow one who went around measuring the Temple and everything else that was destroyed, to say to the people: "God is not done with you or your nation; God is not defeated or done with His plans; God will have future plans for you; Ezekiel's Temple is yet to be built."

Now, after the Roman General (later Emperor) Titus destroyed Herod's Temple, God told John to measure the Temple. The same message is conveyed to God's people in the Church. Don't despair over the Temple. I still have things under control. The Temple may be destroyed, yet it is still with us.

2 And leave out the court which is outside the Temple, and do not measure it, for it has been given to the nations; and they will tread under foot the holy city for forty-two months.

The early church met in the courts outside of the Temple. That's where Jesus taught. That's where Peter and John healed the lame beggar. It's where the Church in Jerusalem worshipped. The Church is going to be given to the nations for forty-two months. This goes back to the answer given after the Saints asked "How long?" Till the number is full. More witnesses are needed.

The forty-two months is another way of saying three and one-half years. Three and a half years symbolizes the Tribulation. $3^1/2$ years = Tribulation.

> 3 And I will grant authority to my two witnesses, and they will prophesy for twelve hundred and sixty days, clothed in sackcloth.

Elijah and John the Baptist wore sackcloth made of coarse camel's hair (2 Kings 1:8; Matt 3:4). Sackcloth was the clothing of one in mourning or anguish. It was also the clothing of prophets (Zechariah 13:4). Twelve hundred and sixty days = $3^1/2$ years = Tribulation.

> 4 These are the two olive trees and the two lampstands that stand before the lord of the earth.

These verses hearken us back to Zechariah 4. The Jews returning from Babylon were trying to rebuild the Temple. There were no great miracles. Zurubbabel, the Governor, and Joshua, the High Priest, did not seem like much in the eyes of the people when they had leaders in their past like Moses and Aaron, David, and Nathan. But in Zechariah, 4 God says they are Mine. They are My witness.

> 5 And if anyone desires to harm them, fire proceeds out of their mouth and devours their enemies; and if anyone would desire to harm them, in this way they must be killed.

Elijah called down fire from Heaven to destroy his enemies (II Kings 1). Yet these witnesses can bring this fire from their mouths. This could symbolize the power of their words.

> 6 These have the power to shut up the sky, in order that rain may not fall during the days of their prophesying; and they have power over the waters to turn them into blood, and to smite the earth with every plague, as often as they desire.

Elijah prayed and it did not rain for three years (I Kings 17:1; 18:1; James 5:17), yet James said it did not rain for $3^1/2$ years; why the difference? In the time between the Old and New Testaments an evil Greek King named Antiochus IV, who called himself Antiochus Epiphanes (god manifest) (Daniel 7:24–28; and the small horn of Daniel Chapter 8), ruled the northern Seleucid Kingdom from 175–164. For $3^1/2$ years he ruled Jerusalem, and tried to make it a Greek nation in thought and religion. From that time on, "$3^1/2$" symbolizes tribulation.

Moses turned water to blood and smote the earth with every plague (Exodus 6–12). This could mean that the witnesses are the true descendants of Moses and Elijah (the Law and the prophets).

> 7 And when they have finished their testimony, the beast that comes up out of the abyss will make war with them, and overcome them and kill them.

We have not been introduced to the beast yet but he is a bad guy. We can tell that much because he kills the two witnesses and he comes up from the abyss. In Chapter 13 we learn that the beast is the Roman Emperor. The death of the two witnesses comes because of the war against Christianity.

8 And their dead bodies will lie in the street of the great city which mystically is called Sodom and Egypt, where also their Lord was crucified.

While the dead bodies are in the street, let us ask the question: who are these two witnesses? The futurists believe that Old Testament saints will come back in the future. Some believe that Enoch and Elijah will come back and do all the things this chapter talks about. Enoch and Elijah are the only ones in the OT who did not die but were taken straight to Heaven. Others believe that it will be Moses and Elijah because what the witnesses do are the same things they did, and Moses and Elijah came back in the New Testament to meet with Jesus (Matt. 17:1–8). Elijah must come back to fulfill Mal. 4:5 that Elijah must come back before the Messiah. Yet Jesus said John the Baptist fulfilled that in Matthew 11:14.

We must come back to the basic question: what did it mean to the Seven Churches? Would they take comfort that in 2,000 years two witnesses will do all these things? I think not. They are under much pressure from the Roman Empire and the local government agencies who want to destroy Christianity. They have already killed all the Apostles except John. As a matter of fact, Nero killed many Christians including Paul and Peter. Peter, an Apostle to the Jews, was with Jesus from the beginning. The gospel of Mark, it is believed, is Mark's recalling what he heard Peter recite to congregation after congregation. Paul, the Apostle to the Gentiles, has helped us to understand the theology of the cross and how we can apply it to our lives without becoming Jewish. Both of these Apostles spoke in Ephesus and would be known to older members. When Nero had them killed it had the effect of saying, we defeated them, and we can defeat Christianity. Many began to wonder if their new religion

116

could survive with the most powerful Empire on earth declaring war on them.

It could be that Peter and Paul are in mind here, yet I think they represent the Jewish and Gentile believers. I believe the two witnesses are Jewish and Gentile believers who find the Empire at war with them. Yet they are the winners. That's what is being said here. If the government takes on Christians for being Christians then they become God's enemy. The Christian wins despite the power of Roman soldiers, and the death they may face.

What city are they in? It could be Rome or Jerusalem; I go for Rome.

9 And those from the peoples and tribes and tongues and nations will look at their dead bodies for three and a half days, and will not permit their dead bodies to be laid in a tomb.

10 And those who dwell on the earth will rejoice over them and make merry; and they will send gifts to one another, because these two prophets tormented those who dwell on the earth.

11 And after the three and a half days the breath of life from God came into them, and they stood on their feet; and great fear fell upon those who were beholding them.

After the Tribulation the world understands who is right. Then people began to name their sons Peter and Paul and name their dogs Nero. During the Tribulation the world hates them but we should expect that.

12 And they heard a loud voice from Heaven saying to them, "Come up here." And they went up to Heaven in the cloud, and their enemies beheld them.

117

Their enemies found out that they spoke for God. They went up to Heaven like Jesus did.

13 And in that hour there was a great earthquake, and a tenth of the city fell; and seven thousand people were killed in the earthquake, and the rest were terrified and gave glory to the God of Heaven.

As soon as they realized that the witnesses spoke for God they should have feared and given glory to God. But no. They had to wait to see for themselves the judgment of God come. Why did they not realize that if these witnesses were from God that they were under the wrath of God, not only for their sins, but what they did to God's men.

14 The second woe is past; behold, the third woe is coming quickly.

15 And the seventh angel sounded; and there arose loud voices in Heaven, saying, "The Kingdom of our world has become the kingdom of our Lord, and of His Christ; and He will reign forever and ever."

The last woe is coming quickly. Jesus will come and judge the world. It is, and has been for 2,000 years, the teaching of the Church that Jesus is coming soon. Right now the Kingdom consists of those who are loyal to the King. All believers are the Kingdom, yet when He comes it is to claim what is His; the world he created.

16 And the twenty-four elders, who sit on their thrones before God, fell on their faces and worshipped God.

17 saying, "We give thanks, O Lord God, the Almighty, who art and who wast, because Thou hast taken Thy great power and hast begun to reign."

The consummation of the ages sets the records straight and gives the elders another reason to praise God. Right now wicked men seem to get by with things (Psalm 73; Job 21). On that great Day of Judgment everything will be put right.

18 And the nations were enraged, and Thy wrath came, and the time came for the dead to be judged, and the time to give their reward to Thy bond-servants the prophets and to the saints and to those that fear Thy name, the small and the great, and to destroy those who destroy the earth.

In this world, those who fear God seem to be on the back of the bus. Not many rich, not many powerful, yet God uses us and is made strong in our weakness. The world hates God and His Kingdom (Psalm 2) but God will quickly overcome all objections and set right what has been wrong for so long. God will reward those who fear Him and have been shunned, demoted, fired, run out of town, burned, crucified, beaten, or killed. He will also destroy those who have made the world so terrible.

19 And the temple of God which is in Heaven was opened; and the ark of His covenant appeared in His temple, and there were flashes of lighting and sounds and peals of thunder and an earthquake and a great hailstorm.

The Temple of God is in Heaven, and that is where the Ark of the Covenant is. The lighting, thunder, earthquake, and hailstorms are all things that make us afraid. The fear of God's Holiness should be stronger than the fear of the natural phenomenon. It's God Holiness that separates us sinful ones from God. Until the sin is dealt with we must keep ourselves at a safe distance. (Exodus 19 & 20)

"I have given them Thy word; and the world has hated them, because they are not of the world, even as I am not of the world."

—John 17:14

"Mr. Ridley, if you will revoke your erroneous opinions, you shall not only have liberty so to do, but also your life."

"Not otherwise?" said Dr. Ridley.

"No," answered Dr. Marshal. "Therefore, if you will not do so, there is no remedy: you must suffer for your deserts."

"Well," said the martyr, "so long as the breath is in my body, I will never deny my Lord Christ and his known truth. God's will be done in me."

They were then commanded to prepare immediately for the stake . . . They then brought a lighted faggot, and laid it at Dr. Ridley's feet, upon which Mr. Latimer said, "Be of good comfort, Mr. Ridley, and play the man! We shall this day light such a candle, by God's grace, in England, as I trust never shall be put out."

—October 1555 *A Tale of Two Martyrs Christian History,* Issue 48, pp. 18–19

12

The Lady

1 And a great sign appeared in Heaven: a woman clothed
with the sun, and the moon under her feet, and on her head
a crown of twelve stars;

We understand this symbolism because Joseph explained it
to us in Genesis 37:9–11. The woman symbolizes the nation
of Israel.

2 and she was with child; and she cried out, being in labor
and in pain to give birth.

Merry Christmas! Now if you want to say the woman is
Mary that's okay also; yet she still symbolizes the nation of
Israel. But we do recognize this as the Christmas story. Just
as this book goes back and forth in place from Heaven to
earth, so too it goes back and forth in time.

3 And another sign appeared in Heaven: and behold, a great
red dragon having seven heads and ten horns, and on his
heads were seven diadems.

4 And his tail swept away a third of the stars of Heaven, and
threw them to the earth. And the dragon stood before the
woman who was about to give birth, so that when she gave
birth he might devour the child.

This is another part of the Christmas story. Satan is the Dragon, and we ill see more of him later. A dragon is a snake with legs. The serpents in Genesis 3 lost their legs but the original serpent still has his. He has seven heads. Now you have heard of someone who was two-faced, or spoke out of both sides of his mouth. Here is someone who has seven different mouths to talk out of. No wonder he is called the author of confusion! While he has seven heads he has ten horns. Are there ten horns on each head or one on four of the heads, and two on three? It is not clear but what is clear is that he has great power. The horn stands for power.

On each head is a crown. He assumes he is king of all. He wants to be king of all. A diadem is a crown you put on that kings wear when they assume power. It's not a crown that you do anything to earn. That this Dragon takes out a third of the stars is symbolic of the Angels who followed Satan when he rebeled against God.

Satan stands before the woman about to give birth. Matthew records this in chapter 2 of his Gospel. It wasn't hard for Satan to figure out when the Messiah would be born. Daniel gave that prophecy in Chapter 9. So Satan made sure that Herod the Great, the powerful King of Israel, who ruled under Rome, would be very paranoid. He was so afraid of losing his kingdom to someone else, he killed his own sons and anyone else that looked like they might have eyes for the throne. When three "Wise Men" came and asked a question of the wrong person, Herod was there to kill Jesus as soon as he appeared. But Jesus was already there a few years before Herod knew he was born. When Herod realized the Wise Men were not going to tell him which child it was, he just killed all the boys of Bethlehem two years and under. Not uncommon for Herod, a man whose paranoia came from a Red Dragon.

5 And she gave birth to a son, a male child, who is to rule all nations with a rod of iron; and her child was caught up to God and to His throne.

The plan to destroy the child did not work. The child grew and completed his mission. In one verse we sidestep all that Jesus did in the Gospels. Yet we know this is Jesus because He is the one to rule the nations with a rod of iron (Psalm 2:9). Jesus is at the right hand of the Throne of God.

6 And the woman fled into the wilderness where she had a place prepared by God, so that there she might be nourished for one thousand, two hundred and sixty days.

Now we saw in verses one and two that the woman could be either Mary or Israel. Now we see that it is true Israel, (Romans 9:6 & 7) believing Israel. The Jewish church flees to the nations as David did when pursued by Saul. One thousand two hundred and sixty days = $3^1/_2$ years = Tribulation.

7 And there was war in Heaven, Michael and his angels were waging war with the dragon. And the dragon and his angels waged war,

Satan is a great and powerful dragon, but he is not all powerful. He is not equal to God. Michael, the only angel mentioned in Revelation by name, and the only one of two in the Bible mentioned by name. His name means "Who is like God?" Perhaps Satan used his name to say he knew who might be like God. Perhaps the zeal of the Lord was upon Michael to answer the blasphemy. Whatever started the war, Michael finished it.

8 and they were not strong enough, and there was no longer a place found for them in Heaven.

9 And the great dragon was thrown down, the serpent of old who is called the devil and Satan, who deceives the whole world; he was thrown down to the earth, and his angels were thrown down with him.

Michael kicked Satan out of Heaven. When this happened we are not told, but when Jesus reports about it, it's in the past tense (Luke 10:8). Satan is a created and defeated being. He was created by God and defeated by Jesus on the cross. His final defeat will come when Jesus comes again. He is called the devil or the slanderer, and Satan the adversary. He is our adversary, not God's. He's against us. He has not the power to be against God. And he has a job. It's the same job he had in the Garden when he disguised himself as a serpent. He deceives the whole world (Eph. 2:2; 6:12;). He cannot take away our salvation, or defeat us or make us sin (James 1:13–15). But he can deceive and confuse.

Being kicked out of Heaven he now comes to earth.

10 And I heard a loud voice in Heaven, saying, "Now the salvation, and the power, and the kingdom of our God and the authority of His Christ have come, for the accuser of our brethren has been thrown down, who accuses them before our God day and night.

There is a rejoicing in Heaven because they got rid of this one who always accuses the brethren with slander. This is what Heaven does with those who are negative all the time.

11 "And they overcame him because of the blood of the Lamb and because of the word of their testimony, and they did not love their life even to death.

At first it sounds like John is going to tell you how the angels overcame Satan, but then he tells us how the saints overcome him. By the blood of the Lamb, what Jesus did on the cross, and the word of their testimony. They were faithful unto death.

12 "For this reason, rejoice, O Heavens and you who dwell in them. Woe to the earth and the sea, because the devil has come down to you, having great wrath, knowing that he has only a short time."

Heaven's gain is our loss. Satan is cast down to earth and now we have to put up with him. The last thing to note about him is that his time is short. His doom is sure and whatever he does he must do quickly.

13 And when the dragon saw that he was thrown down to the earth, he persecuted the woman who gave birth to the male child.

14 And the two wings of the great eagle were given to the woman, in order that she might fly into the wilderness to her place, where she was nourished for a time and times and half a time, from the presence of the serpent.

Now we return to the ongoing story of the struggle going on between Satan and the woman. God helps the woman by giving her wings (Ex. 19:4) to fly off to a safe space for a time (1) and times (2) and half a time ($^1/_2$) $1 + 2 + ^1/_2 = 3^1/_2 =$ Tribulation.

15 And the serpent poured water like a river out of his mouth after the woman, so that he might cause her to be swept away with the flood.

16 And the earth helped the woman, and the earth opened its mouth and drank up the river which the dragon poured out of his mouth.

17 And the dragon was enraged with the woman, and went off to make war with the rest of her offspring, who keep the commandments of God and hold to the testimony of Jesus.

Out of the serpent's mouth comes lies and slander as much as a river. But the earth is the Lord's and the fullness of it. The woman, believing Israel, has offspring, believing Gentiles. To understand who the woman is you must put together all the verses in this chapter (1 & 2, 5 & 6, 13–17). If you took just the first two you would say it was Mary. If you took the last you would say it's the church. It's believing Jews.

If you are an offspring of the woman you have one who wars with you, seeks to deceive you, cause you to sin, defeat you. If you keep the commandments of God and hold to the testimony of Jesus, you have an enemy.

But remember the former days when after being enlightened, you endured a great conflict of sufferings, partly by being made a public spectacle through reproaches and tribulations, and partly by becoming sharers with those who were so treated.

—Hebrews 10:32–33

At two A.M. the bell of St. German l'Auxerrois tolled, at which signal the Duke of Guise led his followers to Coligny's house: the duke remained below while his servants, headed by a young man named Besme, ascended to the admiral's room. After stabbing him (Henry of Navarre, head of the Huguenot princes) several times they threw him out of the window; when his head and arms were cut off by the rabble, and the body hung up by the feet on a gibbet.

The martyrdom of this virtuous man had no sooner taken place then the armed soldiers ran about slaying all the Protestants they could find within the walls of the city. This took place during the first three days, in which above 10,000 men, women, of all ages and conditions, are said to have perished.

These brutal deeds were not confined within the walls of Paris, but extended into other cities and quarters of the realm, especially to Lyons, Orleans, Toulouse, and Rouen, where the cruelties were unparalleled. Within the space of one month 60,000 Protestants are said to have been slain in France alone.

—August, 1572, France *Foxe's Book of Martyrs* p. 83

127

13

The Beast

1 And he stood on the sand of the seashore. And I saw a beast coming up out of the sea, having ten horns and seven heads, and on his horns were ten diadems, and on his heads were blasphemous names.

In verse one we have two main players. The first is the Dragon, or Satan, that we saw in Chapter 12. He stands on the beach to watch with a parent's pride (sort of) someone very much like himself appear.

Like Satan, the Beast has ten horns and seven heads and ten diadems, or crowns he did not earn. The Beast has something added, blasphemous names. The Beast claims to be God.

But who is the Beast? Many identify him with the Antichrist. As we have pointed out, the word Antichrist, which means in place of Christ, is not found in Revelation. Daniel spoke of the little horn, but as we saw earlier, in Chapter 11, v.6, this referred to Antiochus Ephiphanes. Paul spoke about the man of sin, II Thess. 2, but I do not think that Paul was thinking about the Beast but rather the one who would destroy the Temple. Paul knew, because of the prophecy of Jesus that the Temple would be destroyed, that must happen before Jesus came back. It did not happen while Paul was alive, so he knew the lawless man who would destroy the Temple still must come. After Paul died, it was revealed to be Titus, who later became an Emperor. We get the word Antichrist from John who, in his first letter (I John 2:18–22; 4:3), told us that though many are looking for the Antichrist there was no need because there are many antichrists. Why worry so much about someone who may or may not come in our lifetime and ignore all the Antichrists around us? He also told us we are in the last days, and what the doctrine of the Antichrist is. The Antichrist teaches that Jesus is not God. Well, if the Beast, who is an Antichrist (but only one of many), is not the man of sin, or the little horn, who is he?

We can tell from the first verse that he has ten horns. That means he has much power. He has seven heads and, like Satan says, this to one and that to another, he lies like a politician, he has complete crowns; so is in power. And he claims to be god.

> 2 And the beast which I saw was like a leopard, and his feet were like those of a bear, and his mouth like the mouth of a lion. And the dragon gave him his power and his throne and great authority.

In Daniel's dreams about the nations that were to come, the nations were represented by animals. This beast is swift like a leopard, his feet are as big as a bear's, and his mouth is as big as a lion's. The swiftest, the biggest feet, and the biggest mouth. This Beast is a nation that is the most powerful. This Beast is the Roman Emperor. He gets power and authority from the dragon. Now Romans 13 tells us there is no nation in authority that God did not establish. But rather than serve God who gives the Emperor his authority, he serves Satan and takes power from Satan. Romans 13 tells us to obey worldly governments. Revelation 13 tells us that sometimes these governments get the big head, and begin to take on God. When they do, God removes them from power.

129

3 And I saw one of his heads as if it had been slain, and his fatal wound was healed. And the whole earth was amazed and followed after the beast;

This will be explained in greater detail later, but for now all you need to know is that Nero, one of the heads, was the first Emperor to officially persecute the church. The current Emperor Domitian is another Nero. The world follows the power, and the Emperor is the power.

4 and they worshiped the dragon, because he gave his authority to the Beast; and they worshiped the Beast, saying, "Who is like the Beast, and who is able to wage war with him?"

The world worships the Beast but the church is not to worship the Beast. Because God made the Roman Emperor the world power no one can wage war with the Beast.

5 And there was given to him a mouth speaking arrogant words and blasphemies; and authority to act for forty-two months was given to him.

But even though God gave the Emperor the power of a world leader, he did not acknowledge God, but sought power from Satan. He began to say: "I am God." Caesars were all considered gods, but the early ones did not believe it or seek it. The crazy ones like Nero and Caligula insisted on it. Domitian the Emperor (when John wrote Revelation) liked to be addressed as the Most High God.

Forty-two months = $3^1/_2$ years = Tribulation.

6 And he opened his mouth in blasphemies against God, to blaspheme His name and His tabernacle, that is, those who dwell in heaven.

Domitian liked to be called the most High God and that he was the best of Heaven. This is the Beast Revelation is warning the saints of.

> 7 And it was given to him to make war with the saints and to overcome them; and authority over every tribe and people and tongue and nation was given to him.

Now we have no problem with the news that the Beast was given by God to make war with the saints, but what we want to read next is "and the saints overcame him." That, however, is not what we read. We read that God gave him authority over tribes and peoples and tongues and nations and the authority to make war with the saints and overcome them. This was not good news for the first readers of this book. The first readers were facing a losing battle. They found out God has given this evil man and this evil Empire to overcome them.

> 8 And all who dwell on the earth shall worship him, everyone whose name has not been written from the foundation of the world in the book of life of the Lamb who has been slain.

Now listen. Those who worship the Beast are not Christians. Romans want to test the loyalty of the citizens by having everyone burn incense to Caesar's statue and say Caesar is Lord. Those who do that do not have their names written in the Lamb's book of Life. The Lamb of God, Jesus himself, holds the book and those written in it do not worship Caesar.

> 9 If anyone has an ear, let him hear.

Listen, Listen, these are hard sayings.

10 If anyone is destined for captivity, to captivity he goes; if
anyone kills with the sword, with the sword he must be killed.
Here is the perseverance and the faith of the saints.

But if I don't burn incense to Caesar and say Caesar is
Lord, they will put me in prison: . . . then to captivity he
goes. But if I don't burn incense to Caesar and say Caesar
is Lord, the Soldier will kill me with his sword: . . . . with the
sword he must be killed. What is the perseverance of the
saints? Saints persevere by being faithful to Jesus, no matter
who stands in their way. Saints are faithful unto death. The
Government is to be obeyed in those areas where God has
given it authority, according to Romans 13 and I Peter
2:11–17.

11 And I saw another Beast coming up out of the earth; and
he had two horns like a lamb, and he spoke as a dragon.

Now we have another Beast coming up out of the earth
The first Beast came up out of the sea; this Beast comes out
of the earth. There are many ways to understand this, but I
believe you must put yourself back into the place of the first
readers. They lived on the west cost of Asia Minor (what is
now Turkey). If the first Beast was the Roman Emperor, then
he would come from the west, and west of them is the sea.
This Beast is among them. He comes from right there in
Asia Minor. He does not have the ten horns that the first
Beast had, he only has two. He is not that powerful. While
the first one looked like a leopard, lion, and bear; this one
looks like a lamb but he speaks like Satan.

12 And he exercises all the authority of the first Beast in his
presence. And he makes the earth and all those who dwell
in it to worship the first beast, whose fatal wound was healed.

This weak but boastful Beast has the authority of the first Beast when the first Beast is around. The second Beast is the Asiarch, or Ruler, of Asia, the Roman province. Local authorities are always after what we now call federal money. Each city wanted Rome's attention. One way to get that attention is to say our city worships Caesar, and then force compliance on every citizen. Jews of course would be excluded because their religion prohibits idol worship and their religion is recognized by Rome because it existed before the Empire. Christianity as a new religion was not exempt. If you did not burn incense to Caesar and say Caesar is Lord, you were not a loyal citizen. The second Beast makes the earth worship the first Beast.

13 And he performs great signs, so that he even makes fire come down out of heaven to the earth in the presence of men.

14 And he deceives those who dwell on the earth because of the signs it was given to him to perform in the presence of the Beast, telling those who dwell on the earth to make an image to the Beast who had the wound of the sword and has come to life.

Like the Pharaoh in the book of Exodus, the Asiarchs have some magician's tricks to use to whip the worshipers into a frenzy. No matter what the sign is you are not to worship the Roman Emperor. That's the message for the seven churches.

15 And there was given to him to give breath to the image of the Beast, that the image of the Beast might even speak and cause as many as do not worship the image of the beast to be killed.

133

The Greek word for voice is "phony." From that we get the words microphone, telephone, etc. We also get the word phony, which means "not real." It comes from the priest using the ventriloquist's arts to make the dumb idol speak.

The believers are asked to do something that may cost their lives. It's not an easy thing and the cost is up front.

16 And he causes all, the small and the great, and the rich and the poor, and the free men and the slaves, to be given a mark on their right hand, or on their foreheads.

17 and he provides that no one should be able to buy or sell, except the one who has the mark, either the name of the Beast or the number of his name.

Now we come to another mark, the mark of the Beast. We saw earlier the mark of God that kept the judgment of God off of the people of God. With this mark the trade of the city will be used to ensure that every citizen has done his duty, and worshipped Caesar. If every citizen has done his duty the city can report to Rome that they are totally loyal, and get some of that imperial money. The second Beast is the local government that enforces Emperor Worship.

18 Here is wisdom. Let him who has understanding calculate the number of the Beast, for the number is that of a man; and his number is six hundred and sixty-six.

This is probably the most problematic verse in Revelation, not because the riddle cannot be solved but because the riddle can be solved in so many ways. Every public name has been named that can be named with some kind of scheme. Every president and world leader has been found out with someone's misinterpretation. In the last scene of

Indiana Jones: Raiders of the Lost Ark the United States Army was supposed to have the Ark of God that Moses made, in a wooden box. As the soldiers take it away, you think, "Well, now, it's easy to find; just look for a big wooden box." But then they take it into a huge warehouse of big wooden boxes. So many wooden boxes fill the room that one despairs of ever finding it again. That's how I feel about this verse. I believe that the original readers understood this right away but the secret was something going on in A.D. 90. We've lost the simple answer and search for a more difficult one.

The idea is to take the first letter of the alphabet and assign it number 1, the second number 2, etc. Hebrew numbers are done this way. But to answer this riddle, what language do you use? Hebrew, Greek, Latin, or some other language? If seven is the perfect number then six is one short of that, and missing it is sin. Six times three takes it to the superlative.

The best guess comes from David Smith, cited in *Worthy is the Lamb* by Ray Summers (p. 175 ff). He uses Hebrew to add up the words Nron Ksr, which means Nero Caesar. "David Smith adapts this to the Nero redivivus myth. This was an idea current that the wicked Nero was reincarnated in Domitian, who was certainly the ruler at the time of this book."

Come now, you rich, weep and howl for your miseries which are coming upon you . . .

. . . You have condemned and put to death the righteous man; he does not resist you.

—James 5:1–6

Europe had first heard of their existence from Marco Polo about A.D. 1300. The later incursion of the Christian missionaries, the devotion of their converts, and their fierce-fought extermination had been an episode little noticed in Europe. The merciless slaughter of the Christian population, numbering over a quarter of a million, took twenty-four years, and was finished around the year 1638. After this deed Japan plunged into strict seclusion, and had remained almost unknown for many generations. . . . There had been a spell of complete isolation. . . . The arts, culture, and faith of the Japanese had supported a rigid structure of society. Science, machinery, and Western philosophies did not exist for them.

1614–1638, *The Grand Alliance* Winston S. Churchill, p. 579.

14

The Lamb

1 And I looked, and behold the Lamb was standing on Mount Zion, and with Him one hundred and forty-four thousand, having His name and the name of His Father written on their foreheads.

It's hard to look at the evil around us and not get defeated or depressed. Some presentations of Revelation don't teach this lesson and seem at first to praise evil and evil workers. So that won't happen we take a break and remember which side we are on, also which side will win. What could be better in the face of this evil than to see the Lamb, Jesus himself standing on Mount Zion, with his saints. The bad guys are not going to win. Jesus is going to win.

This is a different 144,000 than in chapter 7, because we are talking about something else. In chapter 7 the subject was Jewish believers; here the subject is victory of good over evil; although the symbolism of the number is still the same (12 the people of God × 12 × 1000 a number of greatness). . . . The mark of God is upon these saints. The name of God and Jesus is written on their foreheads. The mark of the beast is not found on them. The name of Father was so holy to the Jews that they would not say the name, and by New Testament times would use euphemisms to speak of God: such as the Holy, the Eternal, etc. The often used phrase "it was given," is a euphemism for "it was given by

God." The Jews to this day call the name God gave to Moses the "unpronounceable name" because they only write, and never speak the holy name. Gentiles would pay Jews to pronounce the name hoping for some magic power. The name of the Father and the Son is on them.

> 2 And I heard a voice from Heaven, like the sounds of many waters and like the sounds of loud thunder, and the voice which I heard was like the sound of harpists playing on their harps.

John hears a voice and gets so caught up in describing what the voice sounds like that he does not tell us what the voice said. It sounds like the voice of Jesus from Chapter 1. It's a big voice. It is loud like many waters, it is loud like thunder, but it is also pretty like harp music. Loud, strong and beautiful, that's what He sounded like as He talked with His saints.

> 3 And they sang a new song before the throne and before the four living creatures and the elders; and no one could learn the song except the one hundred and forty-four thousand who had been purchased from the earth.

Earlier the saints were on Mount Zion; now they are before the throne singing a song only they can sing. They can sing the song because they had been purchased from the earth. They had died for the testimony of Jesus. They were faithful unto death and that is why they sing a song no one else can know.

> 4 These are the ones who have not been defiled with women, for they have kept themselves chaste. These are the ones who follow the Lamb wherever He goes. These have been

purchased from among men as first fruits to God and to the Lamb.

The first part of this verse is as problematic to a married Protestant as it would be for a Jew, for marriage does not defile a man. So this would not mean that they were not married, but rather did not defile themselves with the temple prostitutes. Idol worship was always connected to sexual immorality, and many times in the Old Testament was considered the same thing. These were not celibates who kept themselves from the sin of Eve and her daughters. It was more in line with avoiding the sin of the woman in Chapter 17. Celibacy existed in Greek and Latin traditions but not in Jewish or Christian traditions until later. Rather these kept themselves from idolatry.

They followed the Lamb wherever He went. The Lamb went to a cross. They followed Him even to death. When early Christians faced death they knew they were following their Lord. That's what He did, and death did not stop Him. Death does not defeat a Christian.

Again as in verse three, now in verse four we mention that they are purchased from among men. These are the first fruits, the first ones to face death for witnessing. They will not be the last.

5 And no lie was found in their mouth; they are blameless.

The subject makes us realize we are concerned with a particular lie. When one burnt incense to Caesar he was required to tell a lie, and say Caesar is Lord. But Caesar is not Lord, Jesus is Lord. These Saints would not tell this lie so they were killed in such a way to tell the world that they were criminals. But they were not criminals, they were blameless.

6 And I saw another angel flying in midHeaven, having an eternal gospel to preach to those who live on the earth, and to every nation and tribe and tongue and people;

7 and he said with a loud voice, "Fear God, and give Him glory, because the hour of His judgment has come; and worship Him who made the heaven and the earth and sea and springs of waters."

Now we have the first of three angels flying across the sky with a message for those of us who are on the earth. The first angel has a message of an eternal Gospel that is for the whole world. The Gospel or good news is eternal because the Father and the Son had planned it from before the foundations of the Earth. It was the mystery that was hidden in Old Testament times that the prophets only saw glimpses of. It is the same good news that we will continue to preach till Jesus comes again.

Do not worship Caesar and give him glory, or fear him for he can only kill you. Fear God. His judgment lasts beyond the grave. Only to God does true worship belong. Caesar may rule over much of the earth, but God made the heavens and the earth, the fresh and salt water.

8 And another angel, a second one, followed, saying, "Fallen, fallen is Babylon the great, she who has made all of the nations drink of the wine of the passions of her immorality."

This angel carries a message that is a preview of Chapters 17 & 18. Babylon was a name the Jews had for Rome. Babylon kept the Jews in captivity, and ruled over them. Babylon is gone but Rome is now in her place doing the same thing as Babylon did. Peter writing from Rome sent greetings from the church in Rome by saying "She who is in Babylon . . ." meaning She (the Church) who is in Rome.

Power is heady stuff. When God sets up people to be a world power, it's intoxicating. But Rome could not seem to rule without making the world worship Caesar. That's the immorality. Like a man or woman who is married and has an affair with someone else; the people of God are to stay true to Him. When they worship idols, it's immorality.

9 And another angel, a third one, followed them, saying with a loud voice, "If anyone worships the Beast and his image, and receives a mark on his forehead or upon his hand,

10 he also will drink of the wine of the wrath of God, which is mixed in full strength in the cup of His anger; and he will be tormented with fire and brimstone in the presence of the holy angels and in the presence of the Lamb.

11 "And the smoke of their torment goes up forever and ever; and they have no rest day and night, those who worship the Beast and his image, and whoever receives the mark of His name."

The third angel makes it very clear. If you do not know what to do, whether or not to worship Caesar, we have a message for you. You will be an outlaw of Heaven. God's wrath will fall on you.

12 Here is the perseverance of the saints who keep the commandments of God and their faith in Jesus.

The perseverance of the saints is what divides the "saints" from the "aints." Saints stay faithful to the end. Aints don't. Saints keep the commandments of God, and their faith is in Jesus no matter what the cost. We are not all called on to be martyrs but we are all called upon to be witnesses. And we are to witness even if it costs us our lives.

You may say "Well, I don't know if I could do that." Ask yourself who has your allegiance now? To whom do you belong? To Christ or to the world? Which side are you on? Yes, you have to take sides. This vile world is not a friend of Grace. Saints persevere to the end.

> 13 And I heard a voice from Heaven, saying, "Write 'Blessed are the dead who die in the Lord from now on!' " "Yes," says the Spirit, "that they may rest from their labors, for their deeds follow with them."

In this book God is asking his believers to die for the faith. And so a voice from Heaven tells John "I have a message for those about to die; They are Blessed." The Holy Spirit agrees with this and adds to it. Those who are faithful unto death have rested from their labors and their good deeds are not forgotten, but go with them. The good they did was not for nothing.

> 14 And I looked, and behold, a white cloud, and sitting on the cloud was one like a son of man, having a golden crown on His head, and a sharp sickle in His hand.

This is a harvest vision of the end times. We don't know the identity of the one on the cloud who appears as a son of man. Jesus called himself the Son of Man. This is a son of man. He looks like Jesus; but isn't that the goal, to look like and be like Jesus? On his head he wears a crown. This is not a diadem as the Beast wore, this son of man has earned his (stephanos) crown. I do not believe this is Jesus because he takes orders from an angel, and Jesus said that in the last days angels would do the harvesting (Matt. 13:41)

He has a sharp sickle in His hand to do the job of harvesting the good grain.

15 And another angel came out of the Temple, crying out with a loud voice to Him who sat on the cloud, "Put in your sickle and reap, because the hour to reap has come, because the harvest of the earth is ripe."

16 And He who sat on the cloud swung His sickle over the earth; and the earth was reaped.

When the time is announced from the Father inside the Temple, the harvest begins. Like a good farmer who knows the best time to pick the crops the Father waits until the time is right.

If you were to look to the Book of Revelation as a chronological plan for the future, (which I do not), but if you did; this verse speaks for a mid- or post-tribulation rapture.

Because I do not see the book as an outline of the future events but as comfort to those in tribulation, a look into the future to remind the readers that God and not Rome rules this world and will judge it. All world rulers will be judged by a higher authority. If you want to apply this to a secondary meaning in the future, you may do that but first understand the primary meaning to the first readers.

17 And another angel came out of the Temple which is in Heaven, and he also had a sharp sickle.

18 And another angel, the one who has power over fire, came out from the altar; and he called with a loud voice to him who had the sharp sickle, saying, "Put in your sharp sickle, and gather the clusters from the vine of the earth, because her grapes are ripe."

Now we have a different harvest. In Jesus' parable in Matt. 13 cited above, the harvest was of wheat and tares. Here the harvest involves the good wheat but instead of tares we have grapes for wine. The angel does not come from the inner part of the Temple but from the altar because this angel is in charge of fire.

> 19 And the angel swung his sickle to the earth, and gathered the clusters from the vine of the earth, and threw them into the great wine press of the wrath of God.

> 20 And the wine press was trodden outside the city, and blood came out from the wine press, up to the horses' bridles, for a distance of two hundred miles.

We did not cut, bind, thrash, grind, mix, and bake the wheat, we just harvested it. It's good to be good wheat, so we won't work it over. The grapes are going to be put in a wine press to be trodden out under the feet of others. Judgment comes to the world and the blood will flow. The harvest is a time of fulfillment, a time when all the work on the farm has come to an end and what you've done will be known. The grape harvest stands for the ungodly as it does in Joel 3:13.

Two hundred miles is the length of the pool of blood, but it does not give us the image John wanted to convey because the number has been changed. It should read "sixteen hundred stadia." That Roman measurement adds up to two hundred miles; but it's the number 1,600 we need to understand. The image of 1,600 is 4 (the number of the earth) times four times 100. Basically it is the number of the earth squared and multiplied by 100, not 1,000. God is a God of Grace. 100 represents a great number whereas 1,000 represents the greatest number. $4 \times 4 \times 100 = 1,600$.

The harvest is complete; and what do we have but a simple meal of bread and wine. It is with such a simple meal that Jesus gave to his Church the Lord's Supper as a memorial meal for his broken body and shed blood. But now it has another meaning: that of the final Judgment to come. As this scripture is read in the church the people can look at the altar and see the visual image of the last Judgment to come. Tribulation saints become the bread we understand as the body of Christ. The grape harvest is not the blood of Jesus this time, it is the blood of the unrighteous.

For consider Him who has endured such hostility by sinners against Himself, so that you may not grow weary and lose heart.

—Hebrews 12:3

It was in the year 1814 that John Williams was awakened to spiritual life, by the ministry of the Rev. Timothy East, of Birmingham. From that moment the Gospel wrought a mighty change in his whole nature, so that feeling the powers of the world to come he became a new creature . . . He accordingly offered himself to the London Missionary Society, and was sent to the South Seas . . . 1817 they reached Tahiti . . . We have not the space to narrate the manifold triumphs of the Gospel in the various groups of the South Sea Islands or the adventures of this champion of the cross. He was killed on the 20th of November, 1839, at the island of Erromanga, one of the New Hebrides, whither he had gone to introduce the Gospel.

—November 1839, New Hebrides, *Foxe's Book of Martyrs,* pp. 373–377

15

The Seven Plagues Ready

1 And I saw another sign in Heaven, great and marvelous, seven angels who had seven plagues, which are the last, because in them the wrath of God is finished.

The wrath of God is against Rome and all who attack his church. This is a vision not only of how God feels about his church being attacked but what he is going to do about it.

2 And I saw, as it were, a sea of glass mixed with fire, and those who had come off victorious from the Beast and from his image and from the number of his name, standing on the sea of glass, holding harps of God.

In Chapter 4 there was before the throne a sea of glass, much like the sea Solomon built in front of the Temple (1 Kings 7:23–26). This sea, instead of being water was glass, so Heaven could see what was going on down on earth. This is the image we are working with. Now on that sea before the throne come those who have come through the fire of the judgment of this world. Some of the fire comes with them for they have just died. We are not to feel sorry for them, for they are victors. They refused to worship Caesar. Like David the victorious King, they have harps in their hands to sing praises to God.

3 And they sang the song of Moses the bond-servant of God and the song of the Lamb, saying, "Great and marvelous are

Thy works, O Lord God, the Almighty; Righteous and true are Thy ways, Thou King of the nations.

4 "Who will not fear, O Lord, and glorify Thy name? For Thou alone art holy; for all the nations will come and worship before Thee, for Thy righteous acts have been revealed."

They sang the Song of Moses which is found in Exodus 15. It was the song Moses and the Israelites sang when God saved them from the Egyptians in the Red Sea. God brought forth a great victory and the response was to sing. The people of God sing, and what they sing is of the victory of God, and His mighty deeds. They also sang the song of the Lamb. Which song that is not clear. The people of God still sing many songs that tell of the salvation of the Lamb.

In addition they also say (or sing) that God's works are marvelous and great; that His ways are true and righteous. When you watch governments, you soon realize that not all of their acts are righteous or true. God, not Caesar, is the King of the nations. Caesar must be subject to God, as must all kings of the earth.

Only a fool would refuse to worship God (Psalm 14:1). All the nations, tribes, tongues, and peoples who hear the gospel have those in them that respond to the Righteous God. The Jewish religion is for the Jews. They do not seek converts among the nations. Yet their prophets and psalms speak of a time when all the nations will worship God in Jerusalem.

5 After these things I looked, and the Temple of the tabernacle of testimony in Heaven was opened,

6 and the seven angels who had the seven plagues came out of the Temple, clothed in linen, clean and bright, and girded around their breasts with golden girdles.

148

In response to the saints on the glass sea, who just died for the faith, the Tabernacle opens and seven angels dressed with the same kind of clothing the high priest would wear, come out.

7 And one of the four living creatures gave to the seven angels seven golden bowls full of the wrath of God, who lives forever and ever.

The wrath and Judgment comes not from the saints, or the angels, but from God. His servants have been disgraced (II Samuel 10) and He will respond.

8 And the Temple was filled with smoke from the glory of God and from his power; and no one was able to enter the Temple until the seven plagues of the seven angels were finished.

When God had Moses build the Tabernacle and dedicate it, the Glory of God filled the Tabernacle and they could not enter it. (Exodus 40:34). When Solomon built the Temple, the same thing happened. (I Kings 8:10 & 11) God, by His presence, showed that He was involved with these projects, including this one in v. 8, the wrath in the bowls.

By Faith Moses, when he had grown up, refused to
be called the son of Pharaoh's daughter;

choosing rather to endure ill-treatment with the
people of God, than to enjoy the passing pleasures of
sin;

considering the reproach of Christ greater riches
than the treasures of Egypt; for he was looking to the
reward.

—Hebrews 11:24–26

Queen Ranavalona I, as she titled herself, attacked
the infant church with a fanaticism akin to the Emperor
Nero. She stopped baptisms, banned Scripture, closed
churches, ordered the European missionaries out, and
forbade her subjects, except those in her employ, to
read and write. Her reign of Terror brought her the
name "Bloody Mary of Madagascar."

In 1835 she presented the following charges
against Christians:

1. They despise the idols.
2. They are always praying.
3. They will not swear, but only affirm.
4. Their women are chaste.
5. They are of one mind with regard to their religion.
6. They observe the Sabbath as a sacred day.

—1835 Madagascar—*By Their Blood* by J. & M. Hefly, p. 420

16

The Seven Plagues Poured

1 And I heard a loud voice from the temple, saying to the seven angels, "Go and pour out the seven bowls of the wrath of God into the earth."

2 And the first angel went and poured out his bowl into the earth; and it became a loathsome and malignant sore upon the men who had the mark of the Beast and worshiped his image.

Now God's wrath falls on the men of earth who have oppressed His churches. The sores on the men were like the sore or boils on the Egyptians when God proved he was stronger than all the gods of Egypt. (Exodus 9:8–12)

3 And the second angel poured out his bowl into the sea, and it became blood like that of a dead man; and every living thing in the sea died.

The second bowl is like the plague of blood that came upon the Nile River (Exodus 7:14–25).

4 And the third angel poured out his bowl into the rivers and the springs of waters; and they became blood.

5 And I heard the angel of the waters saying, "Righteous art thou, who art and who wast, O Holy One, because Thou did judge these things;

6 for they poured out the blood of saints and prophets, and Thou hast given them blood to drink. They deserve it.''

7 And I heard the Altar saying, "Yes, O Lord God, the Almighty, true and righteous are Thy judgments.''

The third judgment is like the second yet with fresh water rather than salt. Now we learn that there is an angel of the waters, perhaps an angel to oversee fresh water. Well, now we expect to hear that angel say "Wait a minute! Why are you picking on my water? Judge the land or the sky but leave my water alone.'' That is usually the response we get when someone is in charge of something and that something is threatened, they look out for it: but not this angel. He cares for the things of God. This altar sees why the blood flows like a river because the men on earth made the blood of the saints flow like a river. This angel sees the justice of it all.

The altar agrees or better the ones under the altar from chapter 6:9. They have been waiting to see some justification.

8 And the fourth angel poured out his bowl upon the sun; and it was given to it to scorch men with fire.

9 And men were scorched with fierce heat; and they blasphemed the name of God who has the power over these plagues; and they did not repent, so as to give Him glory.

The next plague brings fire to scorch men with and while it makes believers who were suffering happy it does not have the desired effect on the unbelievers. One would think that if God would just show His power and force these people to stop they would repent and give Him the glory.

They do not. Instead they blaspheme God. If that is the result, should God bring the plague at all?

> 10 And the fifth angel poured out his bowl upon the throne of the beast; and his kingdom became darkened; and they gnawed their tongues because of pain,

> 11 and they blasphemed the God of Heaven because of their pains and their sores; and they did not repent of their deeds.

The fifth bowl corresponds to the plague of darkness sent on Egypt (Exodus 10:21–23). In Egypt this led to fear but no real pain. In this plague the darkness brings great pain, but again no repentance. If this does not bring repentance, maybe another way should be tried. Our goal is to bring the world to repentance, right?

> 12 And the sixth angel poured out his bowl upon the great river, the Euphrates; and its water was dried up, that the way might be prepared for the kings from the east.

The sixth angel brings armies from the east to attack the city of Rome. This brings us to the question: Are these plagues visions of what could be, or did they really happen to the city of Rome? Dr. Summers (p. 159) cites Edward Gibbon as to the reason for the fall of Rome; natural calamity, internal rottenness, and external invasion. Symbolically, all these are represented in the bowls of wrath and the other plagues of this book. But remember, a prophecy—and this book is a prophecy—is understood as conditional. Jeremiah 26 explains that if one repents, God will change his mind. (Jeremiah 26:13 Now therefore amend your ways and your deeds, and obey the voice of the Lord your God; and the Lord will change His mind about the misfortune which He has pronounced against you.) God is always free to change or delay a judgment if there is repentance. By the time that the plagues came, the Christians were praying for Rome and not against her.

> 13 And I saw coming out of the mouth of the dragon and out of the mouth of the Beast and out of the mouth of the false prophet, three unclean spirits like frogs;

> 14 for they are spirits of demons, performing signs, which go out to the kings of the whole world to gather them together for the war of great day of God, the Almighty.

Out of the place of lies come three unclean spirits. Like frogs are unclean and ugly, these three spirits are unclean and ugly. When God speaks people might just repent—so false prophets and lying spirits appear (I Kings 22:21–22). These false spirits work signs so that the Kings of the earth will continue to war with God until that great day when God wins, and the Kings of the earth are defeated.

> 15 ("Behold, I am coming like a thief. Blessed is the one who stays awake and keeps his garments, lest he walk about naked and men see his shame.")

You never know when that day is. Jesus will come back at a time when we do not expect. Stay awake and do not fall into immorality whether spiritually with false religion and even idols, or fleshly with the regular kind of immorality. You may be in some deep darkness when God turns on the light and you will be found out.

> 16 And they gathered them together in the place which in Hebrew is called Har-Magedon.

The Devil, the Emperor, and the Asiarch, and their lying frog-spirits bring the Kings of the earth to be defeated by the living and true God. "Har" is Hebrew for "mountain." Megiddo is a city in the plain of Jezreel. The mountain near Megiddo is Carmel where Elijah faced down and defeated 850 false prophets and proved at a very dark time in Israel's history that GOD is God (I Kings 18).

The Valley below has seen many battles, but the one that stands out in the Bible is found in II Kings 23:28–30. Josiah was Judah's last good King. At Megiddo he went to fight Pharaoh Neco who was on his way to battle the King of Assyria. Neco defeated Josiah, and went on to be defeated by the Assyrians. It was a senseless act, and it was the last time Judah could say there was a good King on the throne of David. It meant the end of Josiah and Judah. To say you will meet your Megiddo could mean the same thing as when we say today "he will meet his Waterloo." A great defeat. What is being said is that the Kings of the Earth who war with God will be defeated.

> 17 And the seventh angel poured out his bowl upon the air; and a loud voice came out of the Temple from the throne, saying, "It is done."

The angel poured out the last bowl of Judgment and the voice coming from God's throne is relieved that it is the last Judgment from God. When Jesus received the judgment for our sins on the cross, three Gospels tell us that "Jesus called out with a loud voice," but only John tells us what He said. Jesus said "It is finished" (John 19:30). While it sounds the same, the words are different in Greek. Jesus completed the plan of the ages in his death on the cross and fulfilled the Law and the Prophets. Here it is the simple word to mean it is done. In both the Judgment of God comes to an end. God does not delight in the death of the wicked.

18 And there were flashes of lightning and sounds and peals of thunder; and there was a great earthquake, such as there has not been since man came to be upon the earth, so great an earthquake was it, and so mighty.

The pouring out of the bowl ended the Judgments of God but the effects were still to happen. The judgment comes to earth in the form of a storm, and an earthquake.

19 And the great city was split into three parts, and the cities of the nations fell. And Babylon the great was remembered before God, to give her the cup of the wine of His fierce wrath.

Rome must stand before God for the saints she put to death. Even so many nations have been judged and will be judged for the way they treat God's people. The Cup of Wrath was introduced to us in Jeremiah 25:15–38.

20 And every island fled away, and the mountains were not found.

21 And huge hailstones, about one hundred pounds each, came down from heaven upon men; and men blasphemed God because of the plague of the hail, because its plague was extremely severe.

There is no place to hide from the judgment of God. The last plague has hail the size of a talanton: an old weight that weighs any where from 108–130 lbs. (A. T. Robertson, *Word Pictures in the New Testament Vol. VI*, p. 427) Egypt felt the hail as a judgment from God but not this big. (Exodus 9:22–26)

The effect of the plagues did not bring repentance from the men; instead they blasphemed God. Perhaps just immediate judgment like the seven Churches wanted to see is not best, but in God's time it came.

By faith he left Egypt, not fearing the wrath of the king; for he endured, as seeing Him who is unseen.

—Hebrews 11:27

Suspected Christians were arrested. Sixteen hundred pleaded guilty to the queen's charges. Those who refused to worship the idols to which the queen prayed were chained in dungeons or killed. To the frustration of the mad ruler, for every Christian put to death, a score of new believers sprang up to take their place.

Fifteen of the group were to be hurled over a high cliff into a rocky ravine 150 feet below. The idols were taken to the top of the cliff and as each victim was lowered a little over the precipice, the demand was made, "Will you worship your Christ or the queen's gods?" Each answered "Christ." As the ropes were cut, the martyrs plunged downward, some singing as they fell.

Only one of the fifteen was spared, a young girl who was declared insane and sent to a distant village. She lived to establish a large church in the community and to win her relatives to Christ.

—1849, Madagascar, *By Their Blood,* by J. & M. Hefly, p. 420–421

17

The Other Woman

1 And one of the seven angels who had the seven bowls came and spoke with me, saying, "Come here, I shall show you the judgement of the great harlot who sits on many waters,

2 with whom the kings of the earth committed acts of immorality, and those who dwell on the earth were made drunk with the wine of her immorality."

The judgment of Rome has been shown and now we see another view of the same thing. In this vision we see things as they are, with a view of how it will be. To the Prophets, immorality did not just mean sexual impurity, although that was involved, but meant that Israel had been untrue to Her true husband God, and followed after false gods. (Hosea) Idol worship many times involved sexual immorality also.

This harlot is not just sitting on one city next to one body of water, but many cities next to many waters. The water also symbolizes many people (v. 15). This harlot has sinned with the Kings that she made drunk with her special brew.

3 And he carried me away in the Spirit into a wilderness; and I saw a woman sitting on a scarlet beast, full of blasphemous names, having seven heads and ten horns.

The wilderness is where the evil things are (Matthew 4:1). The harlot is riding a familiar beast, in fact it is the emperor himself whom we saw earlier in Chapter 13.

4 And the woman was clothed in purple and scarlet, and adorned with gold and precious stones and pearls, having in her hand a cup full of abominations and of the unclean things of her immorality,

5 and upon her forehead a name was written, a mystery, "BABYLON THE GREAT, THE MOTHER OF HARLOTS AND OF THE ABOMINATIONS OF THE EARTH."

6 And I saw the woman drunk with the blood of the saints, and with the blood of the witnesses of Jesus. And when I saw her I wondered greatly.

The woman is rich. She wears purple and scarlet, gold and precious stones and pearls. Immorality has been very, very good for her (Psalm 73). Her cup is full of unclean things in addition to the fact that she is drunk with the blood of the saints. Her name is on the forehead, where everyone wears either the mark of God, or the mark of the Beast.

7 And the angel said to me, "Why do you wonder? I shall tell you the mystery of the woman and of the Beast that carries her, which has the seven heads and the ten horns.

8 "The beast that you saw was and is not, and is about to come up out of the abyss and to go to destruction. And those who dwell on the earth will wonder, whose name has not been written in the book of life from the foundation of the world, when they see the Beast, that he was and is not and will come."

9 Here is the mind which has wisdom. The seven heads are seven mountains on which the woman sits,

The angel does not want anyone confused. The city of Rome has been riding the wild ride of the soap opera that has been the Imperial Palace. She has enjoyed the spoils of the Empire and she bears the guilt. The mind of wisdom was needed in Chapter 13 to understand the number 666, and whatever that used to mean is lost to us, but now we have another chance to identify this monster with the seven heads. The city of Rome sits on seven hills. The hills are one of the identifying mark of this Beast, but the seven heads have another meaning. It speaks of an event that causes all the world who are not saved by the blood to wonder.

10 and they are seven kings; five have fallen, one is, the other has not yet come; and when he comes he must remain a little while.

11 And the beast which was and is not, is himself also an eighth, and is one of the seven, and he goes to destruction.

One is not and is; what does all this mean? Well it is not as hard as it sounds. Let's start with

The Roman Emperors

1. Augustus   27 B.C. to A.D. 14
2. Tiberius   14 to 37
3. Caligula   37 to 41
4. Claudius   41 to 54
5. Nero   54 to 68
    Gilba   68 to 69

Otho	69
Vitellius	69
6. Vespasian	69 to 79
7. Titus	79 to 81
8. Domitian	81 to 96

Notice on this list that three of the Emperors are not counted. After the death of Nero there was a struggle for power that Vespasian finally won. Gilba, Otho, and Vitellius sat on the throne for a few months before each fell in order but would have made no different to the provinces such as Asia where the seven churches are. The seven churches would only recognize or know about the ones I have numbered. They are the only ones who count.

Nero was the fifth Emperor, and had a very interesting reign. Nero was crazy, not as crazy as Caligula, but then again who is. In the first half of his reign Nero had some very capable men around him so that the Empire ran well despite the one on the throne. Now, it always takes a long time for laws and the effects of an Emperor's rule to get to the people. Half way through his reign Nero killed his handlers. In the last half of his reign it was the real Nero ruling, but by the time the effects of that rule hit the people, Nero was killed. So from far out in the Empire, it seemed that Nero was a great leader. Nero was also the first Caesar to persecute Christians for being Christians. He would strap Christians to poles and set them on fire and use them as torches for his garden parties.

When Domitian began to persecute Christians, people wondered if Nero was back on the throne. Nero was seen in the hinterlands as being so great that he could not be dead, but rather merely hiding, waiting to come back. This is the Nero Revesus Myth. The Myth is used here to identify Caesar as the Beast.

12 "And the ten horns which you saw are ten kings, who have not yet received a kingdom, but they receive authority as kings with the Beast for one hour.

13 "These have one purpose and they give their power and authority to the Beast.

The Empire is made up of many (10) Kingdoms who serve under the Emperor. To keep their jobs they show allegiance to Caesar.

14 "These will wage war against the Lamb, and the Lamb will overcome them, Because He is Lord of lords and King of kings, and those who are with Him are the called and chosen and faithful."

The Kings of the earth, the local Kings, Governors, (in the case of the seven Churches, the Asiarchs, or the Rulers of Asia), in order to prove allegiance to Rome would promote Emperor worship, and persecute anyone who would not go along. It has been understood in history that Domitian persecuted the churches. The indication is that most of the persecution was from the local authorities.

The persecution of the church is an attack on Jesus himself. (Acts 9:5) Jesus wins the war. You may die in a battle but the war will be won. Your job is to be faithful.

15 And he said to me, "The waters you saw where the harlot sits, are peoples and multitudes and nations and tongues.

16 "And the ten horns you saw, and the Beast, these will hate the harlot and make her desolate and naked, and will eat her flesh and will burn her up with fire.

17 "For God has put it in their hearts to execute His purpose by having a common purpose, and by giving their kingdom to the Beast, until the words of God should be fulfilled.

18 "And the woman who you saw is the great city, which reigns over the kings of the earth."

The city that has made so much money, and has enjoyed the wealth of the world, also has their envy. At the same time that they make their allegiance they hate losing all their money. Some day they will help with Rome's demise. Until that time they will smile and pay up.

And indeed, all who desire to live godly in Christ Jesus will be persecuted.

—2 Timothy 3:12

"It was late when he left his friends and started upon his lone journey to that once happy home. The long ride of forty miles consumed the remainder of one night, and in the early dawn he alighted at his own house. A hurried interview with his beloved wife, at which they were seen in tears, greatly agitated, was cut short by calls for him to see the sick. On November 29, 1847, immediately after dinner, perhaps about half-past one, the carnage was begun and continued for eight days." The first to die was (Missionary to the Native Americans in Oregon) Dr. Marcus Whitman. Of the seventy-two persons at his (missionary) station, fourteen were massacred. Almost all the others were imprisoned by the Indians. "Nearly fifty persons, mostly women and children, were taken prisoners by them, the women being subjected to horrible abuse."

—November, 1847, *Heroes of the Cross,* by Don O. Shelton

18

Fall of Babylon

1 After these things I saw another angel coming down from Heaven, having great authority, and the earth was illuminated with his glory.

This angel has such great authority that he lights up the whole world. When Moses was in the presence of God his face shone with the reflection of God's Glory. This angel is very close to God.

2 And he cried out with a mighty voice, saying, "Fallen, fallen is Babylon the great! And she has become a dwelling place of demons and a prison of every unclean spirit, and a prison of every unclean and hateful bird.

3 "For all the nations have drunk of the wine of the passion of her immorality, and the kings of the earth have committed acts of immorality with her, and the merchants of the earth have become rich by the wealth of her sensuality."

The mighty angel pronounced the same judgment on the New Babylon (Rome) that fell on Old Babylon (Isaiah 21:9). Rome was called Babylon by Jews because they felt just as captive under Rome as they had under Babylon (1 Peter 5:13). As the Old Babylon has become a city without people, so would Rome. (Jeremiah 51:37). The birds are called out to eat the defeated armies (1 Samuel 17:46).

What this city has done was not done alone. Her wealth has bought her friends to whom she taught her immorality. She would pass out the drinks and the Kings of the earth would drink with her (Jeremiah 51:7). The merchants of the earth got rich serving her desires. What would these Kings and merchants do if Babylon fell?

4 And I heard another voice from Heaven, saying, "Come out of her, my people, that you may not participate in her sins and that you may not receive of her plagues;

5 for her sins have piled up as high as Heaven, and God has remembered her iniquities."

God's people are commanded to come out of Rome just as Jesus warned Christians to flee Jerusalem (Matt: 24). Flee because they might sin with her. We are to be in the world and not of the world. But even if you do not sin you will receive the plagues because there are so many of them.

Prophecy is a warning; if you do not repent, God will bring a plague upon you. If you do repent, the plague will be taken away—or at least put off till later. In this case Christians did not abandon Rome or cease to pray for her. While the judgments of God did fall on Rome (at one point it was only Christians who were left in Rome) the judgments of God came later and over a longer period of time. Rome is still a city, but it is known in the world not as a great power but as the home of a church she once persecuted.

6 "Pay her back even as she has paid, and give back to her double according to her deeds; in the cup which she has mixed, mix twice as much for her."

The judgment on Rome is determined by Rome. As you attack the church you will receive twice the evil back.

167

7 To the degree that she glorified herself and lived sensuously, to the same degree give her torment and mourning; for she says in her heart, "I sit as a queen and I am not a widow, and will never see mourning."

The sins of arrogance and pride do not go unnoticed by Heaven. No Nation anywhere can say, "this will never happen to me."

8 "For this reason in one day her plagues will come, pestilence and mourning and famine, and she will be burned up with fire; for the Lord God who judges her is strong.

The rottenness of Rome will cause the city to fall one day. The false front and new paint that hide the rottenness in the wood cause the building to come down in one day while everyone thought it would stand forever.

9 "And the kings of the earth, who committed acts of immorality and lived sensuously with her, will weep and lament over her when they see the smoke of her burning,

10 standing at a distance because of the fear of her torment, saying, 'Woe, woe, the great city, Babylon, the strong city! For in one hour your judgment has come.' "

The first group to notice the smoke of her burning is her old drinking buddies. They do not come running to help lest they too receive the judgments of God. During England's finest hour in World War II, when Hitler had taken all of Europe and was bombing and threatening to cross the Channel to claim the British Isles as well, Winston Churchill called on all colonies of the British Empire past and present to come to the aid of Mother England. The amazing thing is that they did. The usual thing is for us to stand aside and say tsk, tsk, that is just awful. Just as Rome's old drinking buddies did.

11 And the merchants of the earth weep and mourn over her, because no one buys their cargoes anymore;

12 cargos of gold and silver and precious stones and pearls and fine linen and purple and silk and scarlet, and every kind of citron wood and every article of ivory and every article made from very costly wood and bronze and iron and marble,

13 and cinnamon and spice and incense and perfume and frankincense and wine and olive oil and fine flour and wheat and cattle and sheep, and cargoes of horses and chariots and slaves and human lives.

The second group at the funeral of Rome are the merchants. Those wonderful people that are our dear friends because we shop at their store. These folks are really upset because they lost a good customer. We even get a look at the shopping list and see quite an abundance of things. A few are necessities, like foods that in earlier days did not need to be imported, but were found in abundance in Italy's fertile valleys. Yet, with a growing Empire's more important desk jobs, few Italians wanted to stay on the farms. Only the unproductive farms of Senators' families were found in Italy in Rome's last days, so that even the necessities needed to be imported.

Most of the list is made up of luxurious things that we think we need, but don't. The last two items are disturbing to modern ears—we don't like to think of slavery in these modern times, yet today in the Sudan Christians are sold as slaves. It could even be argued that minimum wage is a form of slavery, if not a direct affront to God (Malachi 3:5).

In America we traffic in the souls of men all the time. From pornography to religious hucksters who sell out for money, we trade in the souls of men and stand in the way of the same judgment from God.

14 And the fruit you long for has gone from you, and all things that were luxurious and splendid have passed away from you and men will no longer find them.

15 The merchants of these things, who became rich from her, will stand at a distance because of the fear of her torment, weeping and mourning,

The merchants do not come running to help their dear friend in the time of need, but like the Kings of the earth they stay at a safe distance. Their biggest fear is that they will never find such a good customer as Rome.

16 saying, "Woe, woe, the great city, she who was clothed in fine linen and purple and scarlet, and adorned with gold and precious stones and pearls;

17 for in one hour such great wealth has been laid waste!" And every shipmaster and every passenger and sailor, and as many as make their living by the sea, stood at a distance.

18 and were crying out as they saw the smoke of her burning, saying, "What city is like the great city?"

19 "And they threw dust on their heads and were crying out, weeping and mourning, saying, "Woe, woe, the great city, in which all who had ships at sea became rich by her wealth, for in one hour she has been laid waste!"

The last group are the sailors, shipmasters and those who love sea travel; for Rome made the Mediterranean Sea a safe and prosperous waterway for commerce. The swift ships of the Mediterranean Sea do not rush to the aid of the city as she burns. They stay at a swift distance and weep over the loss of their money.

20 "Rejoice over her, O heaven, and you saints and apostles and prophets, because God has pronounced judgment for you against her."

Not everyone is sad to see the old city go. Heaven can rejoice. Apostles, such as Peter and Paul who were killed in Rome, can rejoice that God's judgment declares they were not common criminals and Rome is wrong to judge them so. Rome is right to execute murderers and criminals who do harm to the innocent, as an agent of God for good (Romans 13:1–7). But Rome incurred the wrath of God by attacking God's people for no reason.

21 And a strong angel took up a stone like a great millstone and threw it into the sea, saying, "Thus will Babylon, the great city, be thrown down with violence, and will not be found any longer."

In Psalm 2 an image of breaking a vase with an iron rod is used to show how God and His Messiah will judge and overpower strong nations. Now in another demonstration a mill stone is thrown down with a great splash into the sea, to disappear in deep darkness.

22 "And the sound of harpists and musicians and flute players and trumpeters will not be heard in you any longer; and no craftsman of any craft will be found in you any longer; and the sound of a mill will not be heard in you any longer;

23 and the light of a lamp will not shine in you any longer; and the voice of the bridegroom and bride will not be heard

171

in you any longer; for your merchants were the great men of the earth, because all the nations were deceived by your sorcery."

The regular sounds of the city will not continue, while you disregard God and attack the people of God without a reason. The sorcery of emperor worship has gone out to all the earth to deceive, making good evil and evil good.

24 "And in her was found the blood of prophets and of saints and of all who have been slain on the earth."

The catacombs under Rome still speak of the saints who have been slain. God will not sit still and let this happen without sending His judgment.

The Spirit Himself bears witness with our spirit that are children of God,

and if children, heirs of God and fellow-heirs with Christ, if indeed we suffer with Him in order that we may also be glorified with Him.

—Romans 8:16–17

"Christian Erh Mao Tsu!" they shouted.

"Followers of the foreign devils!"

They crowded around Pastor Chen (Wei-Ping) and his family, yelling and pushing them toward the Buddhist temple. The eleven-year-old girl began to cry, but the other four faced their tormentors with dry-eyed faith.

At the temple the leader of the Boxers slapped Pastor Chen across the face, demanding that he kowtow to the idol.

Pastor Chen drew away from the ruffian and with the decisiveness of faith answered, "I have been a Christian for 33 years and have never worshiped idols. I will not begin now."

"Christians!" The Boxers shrieked, "Kill them! Take them to the market place that the villagers may see what happens to those who worship foreign gods."

The Boxers pushed the five Christians toward the center of the village, a shrieking, jeering crowd gathering as they went along. There, the Boxers began a loud, off-key chant, circling the Christians. One of the Boxers took his sword, swung it over his head, slashed the pastor's neck and the right side of his breast, killing him.

The little girl clung to her mother, crying, "What shall we do?"

Chen Ti Ti put her arm around her daughter and comforted her. "We will all go up together to meet our Saviour, our God."

A Boxer thrust his long spear into the back of the little girl with such force that it went clear through her and into the breast of her mother, murdering them both.

A third chopped off the head of the seventeen-year-old boy, and a fourth man cut down the guide. In a matter of seconds five Christians died for their faith!

—June, 1900, *In Spite of Dungeon,* Dorothy C. Haskin, Zondervan Publishing House, 1962, pp. 36–37.

19

Hallelujah!!

1 After these things I heard, as it were, a loud voice of a great multitude in heaven, saying, "Hallelujah! Salvation and glory and power belong to our God;

2 because His judgments are true and righteous; for He has judged the great harlot who was corrupting the earth with her immorality, and He has avenged the blood of his bond-servants on her."

This is a chapter of Worship. It begins with a great multitude in Heaven who give God a three-fold doxology for the work He has done in judging Rome. No nation or world power can afford to attack the bond-servants of God, for God takes it personally.

3 And a second time they said, "Hallelujah! Her smoke rises up forever and ever."

As they see the smoke rise up, the same group gives out another Hallelujah. Rome is in ruins and the ruins can still be seen. She will never again be a world power.

4 And the twenty-four elders and the four living creatures fell down and worshiped God who sits on the throne saying, "Amen. Hallelujah!"

Now the inner circle gets involved. They agree with the great multitude by saying Amen. They fall down before God and worship Him. They give praise to God by saying Hallelujah!

5 And a voice came from the throne, saying, "Give praise to our God, all you His bond-servants, you who fear Him, the small and the great."

Now a voice comes from the throne, which is not God and not the throne. Sometimes statements come from the White House, that are not from the President per se but are from the White House. This voice calls for more praise.

6 And I heard, as it were, the voice of a great multitude and as the sound of many waters and as the sound of mighty peals of thunder, saying, "Hallelujah! For the Lord our God, the Almighty reigns."

Now a greater multitude, all the bond-servents of God, enter into the worship service. Their voice is very loud, and they are celebrating the fact that God is in control and not evil.

7 "Let us rejoice and be glad and give the glory to Him, for the marriage of the Lamb has come and His bride has made herself ready."

The defeat of evil is not the only reason to rejoice. There is a wedding to attend. In the Old Testament the people of God are seen as the Bride of God, but always in an unfaithful way (Hosea 1–3). In the New Testament Paul gives instruction for husbands and wives (Ephesians 5:21–33) and mingles that instruction with the idea that husbands and wives mirror the relationship of Christ and the Church. Now nowhere does it come out and say that the Church is the Bride of Christ, but that clearly is the implication.

The placing of the wedding announcement here does not mean that the wedding is taking place just before the Beast is destroyed. The wedding is yet future, for all the guests have not made themselves ready. The announcement is here to inspire the guests to make the linen.

8 And it was given to her to clothe herself in fine linen, bright and clean; for the fine linen is the righteous acts of the saints.

The righteous acts of the saints are no longer filthy rags because they are filled with the Holy Spirit, and are doing the work of the Father by the Grace of Christ. These are not self-centered acts to make ourselves look good. This is the work of God done by his bond-servants. The purpose of writing this book is to encourage Christians to do good works in hard times. To keep the Testimony of Jesus even if it means death.

9 And he said to me, "Write, 'Blessed are those who are invited to the marriage supper of the Lamb.' " And he said to me, "These are the true words of God."

The Angel does not want John to miss the point. Believers are invited to join God, and those who in obedience keep their testimony can be a part of that. They are blessed if they are invited, this is the true word of God.

10 And I fell at his feet to worship him. And he said to me, "Do not do that; I am a fellow servant of yours and your brethren who hold the testimony of Jesus; worship God. For the testimony of Jesus is the spirit of prophecy."

177

John is so taken with the angel who gives him the message that he makes the mistake of angel worship. Angel worship was a mistake that happened in the first century and happens today. The reflection of the Glory of God makes the already dazzling appearance of an angel more important to a mere mortal. The angel is a true angel and knows that worship only belongs to God.

The testimony of Jesus is what the Book of Revelation is about. The question before the believers is this: should they keep the testimony, or should they say they do not know Him, as Peter did? It was a mistake Peter regretted, and after he was restored he did not repeat that mistake. They must, we must, keep the testimony of Jesus even in the face of death.

The Testimony of Jesus is the Spirit of Prophecy. It is what prophecy is all about. It is what the Prophets were talking about and wished to see. That Jesus died for our sins on the cross and rose from the dead is the center of prophecy, not the future. There is a future, but that is not the Spirit of Prophecy. The cross of Jesus, the Testimony written on every heart of every believer is.

11 And I saw Heaven opened; and behold, a white horse, and He who sat upon it is called Faithful and True; and in righteousness He judges and wages war.

Now the object of worship comes forth to stop the evil that is on the earth. He is the Good Guy on the White Horse. He was faithful even unto death. He is True Son of God. In this world men judge and wage war for personal gain or pride or love of war. Jesus wages war in righteousness. The war has been going on; He comes now to stop it.

12 And His eyes are a flame of fire, and upon His head are many diadems; and He has a name written upon Him which no one knows except Himself.

His eyes have that same look they did in Chapter 1:14. On His head are many crowns or diadems. All authority has been given to Him (Matt. 28:18). The Holy Name of God (Exodus 3:14–15) has been lost (as to how to pronounce the Name), the name Jesus has is so Holy only He knows it.

13 And He is clothed with a robe dipped in blood; and His name is called The Word of God.

He is called the Word of God (John 1:1). And He has a robe dipped in blood. Whose blood is it? Is it the blood of Jesus Himself that He shed for us? Is it the blood of His enemies? Is it the blood of the saints who have died and He welcomed home? A good case has been made for all of these, and all of these give us a true view of Jesus. It is by His blood that we are redeemed. He would wear with pride the blood of the saints to battle to show everyone why He is there. He is the one to execute judgment on anyone who attacks the church (Isaiah 63:1–6). While the executor of God's wrath fulfills the Old Testament, I still like all three ideas.

14 And the armies which are in Heaven, clothed in fine linen, white and clean, were following Him on white horses.

We are not told if the armies are angels or saints. The Lord of Hosts always assumes an angelic army, yet the linen suggests saints. Whoever they are (I prefer saints), they are clean and not blood-stained like their leader. They are here to witness a battle and not to fight in one. The battle is the Lord's.

15 And from His mouth comes a sharp sword, so that with it He may smite the nations; and He will rule them with a rod of iron; and He treads the wine press of the fierce wrath of God, the Almighty.

Out of His mouth comes the same sharp two-edged sword John found in Chapter 1:16. This sharp sword is the word of God. God destroys sinners with the word and raises them up to newness of life. This is, you see, the battle. Till He comes again, He smites the nations looking for any who will repent. When he comes again those who would not be redeemed will be dealt with, and He will break them as an iron rod breaks a vase (Psalm 2). He will judge the nations in history, and at the end of history the wrath of God will tread the evil ones as people stomp on grapes (Isaiah 63:1–6).

16 And on His robe and on His thigh He has a name written, "KING OF KINGS, AND LORD OF LORDS."

The identity of Jesus is on his robe, but if He is passing by and you are standing on the ground you may not be able to read what is on his robe. You can read what is written on His thigh. He is the King of the Kings of the earth and anywhere else. He is King of all Kings. He judges Kings when they get out of line, and they do. He is Lord of Lords. He judges all who lord it over others. He has authority over Presidents, Prime Ministers, Kings, Emperors, Potentates, Tyrants, and thugs (like Hitler) who for a short time grab power. He is Ruler and Judge of all. We are to obey worldly rulers but remember that He is over them.

17 And I saw an angel standing in the sun; and he cried out with a loud voice, saying to all the birds which fly in mid-Heaven, "Come, assemble for the great supper of God;

180

18 in order that you may eat the flesh of kings and the flesh of commanders and the flesh of mighty men and the flesh of horses and of those who sit on them and the flesh of all men, both free men and slaves, and small and great.''

This will be a great battle, and great battles (I Samuel 17:44, 46) begin with an invitation to the birds to feed on the dead. This is a warning to the enemy that he will lose. The Great Roman Empire is at war with a scattered collection of churches that are peaceful, and unarmed. The Roman Empire hasn't got a chance. Whatever you have to throw at the church the birds can eat.

19 And I saw the Beast and the kings of the earth and their armies, assembled to make war against Him who sat upon the horse, and against His army.

20 And the Beast was seized, and with him the false prophet who performed the signs in his presence, by which he deceived those who had received the mark of the Beast and those who worshiped his image; these two were thrown alive into the lake of fire which burns with brimstone.

The Roman Emperor is cast into the lake of fire, and so are the rulers of Asia who promoted emperor worship. It is not a hard thing for Jesus to do. When He is ready these blasphemers will be quickly done with.

21 And the rest were killed with the sword which came from the mouth of him who sat upon the horse, and all the birds were filled with their flesh.

The word of God is there to redeem or condemn any who oppose the Son of God.

Consider it all joy, my brethren, when you encounter various trials,

knowing that the testing of your faith produces endurance.

And let endurance have its perfect result, that you may be perfect and complete, lacking in nothing.

—James 1:2–4

Rufus Gray was among a group of Southern Baptist missionaries from China interned in the Philippines. He and his wife had been attending language school when the Japanese overran Peking.

Soon after arriving in the Philippines Gray was taken in for questioning. His wife and friends never saw him again, nor was his body ever recovered.

His hobby was photography and he had taken hundreds of pictures in Peking. The Japanese may have assumed that he was a spy.

—WWII, The Philippines, *By Their Blood* by J. & M. Hefley, p. 192)

20

The Plan

1 And I saw an angel coming down from Heaven, having the key of the abyss and a great chain in his hand.

The angel who holds the key of the abyss is not from below but from above. God dominates not only Heaven and Earth but Hell as well. Satan is allowed to rule for a short time only. God has those days numbered, and when he says so Satan's judgment will come. Satan does not have the key to the abyss. He does not rule in Hell; he is thrown in just like anyone else. The angel has a great chain that can do the job that needs to be done.

2 And he laid hold of the dragon, the serpent of old, who is the devil and Satan, and bound him for a thousand years,

This angel does not war with Satan, there is no struggle. The Evil One is arrested like a common street thug. One angel, not an archangel, can quickly overpower and arrest Satan; all that is needed is the word.

Four names appear for the same person. He is the dragon of the Book of Revelation, we have seen the damage he has done in this book and the war he has waged on the churches. He was the power behind the two beasts, but now they are in the Lake of Fire. Heaven can no longer let the Dragon walk the streets. We have seen the evil the Dragon has done in this book.

This Dragon in the last book of the Bible is the same snake that is in the first book of the Bible. He did not make Adam and Eve sin, any more than he made the Roman Empire persecute Christians, or worship the Emperor. James tells us of his limitations in James 1:14. Satan entices us to do what we want to do anyway. He has always been against the people of God.

He is also known as the Devil. "Devil" is a Greek word for slander, of false accuser. Jesus told us that he is a liar from the beginning (John 8:44). He slanders God and His Word, and He slanders God's people.

The last alias given here is Satan, which means "Accuser." He is the accuser of the brethren. He is the prosecuting attorney who is always attacking Christians. Many times he has willing accomplices in the church. We are too ready to accuse a brother and do the devil's work, thinking we are doing the work of God. Jesus told us about the devil in John 8:44 ". . . He was a murderer from the beginning, and does not stand in the truth, because there is no truth in him. Whenever he speaks a lie, he speaks from his own nature; for he is a liar, and the father of lies."

This is the first time that the thousand years or the millennium is mentioned. The thousand years is mentioned six times in six verses (19:2–7). Before these verses nothing is ever said about the thousand years and after these verses nothing is said about them. Very few things are told to us about the thousand years because the people reading this may not live to see it. In the next section I will discuss this more fully, here I only want to give it the space and importance that is given in Revelation itself. The first thing we can say is that after a time of tribulation, Satan will be bound for a thousand years. The Seven Churches were in the Tribulation as this is written, after that is the Millennium.

3 and threw him into the abyss, and shut it and sealed it over him, so that he should not deceive the nations any longer, until the thousand years were completed; after these things he must be released for a short time.

Not only will Satan be bound by a chain, he will be thrown into the abyss and locked up. Now we are told why he is locked up: so that he will not deceive the nations any longer. Satan lies to the nations about the church, God, salvation, God's Word. The church that is trying to reach the world has to spread the Gospel while at the same time a very powerful liar is spreading misinformation. God's truth is getting out but with much opposition. For a thousand years the church is free to tell the truth without this interference.

When the thousand years are over, the adversary will be released for a short time and the church will have to deal again with more lies. The short time must be seen from the perspective not only of Heaven but also from those still in the Tribulation. The first readers are a thousand years plus from this "short time." It is called a short time because it is a time period that they do not need to know a lot about. The distant future to them is really unimportant. Do you really care what is going to happen, after a thousand years go by, when the present is filled with war? They have problems now, and so if Satan is released for another thousand or two or five thousand years, it's still a short time. He will be judged like the Beast and the false prophet. He only has a short time to tell his lies and misinform people and lead them to their deaths. To us, that short time is important because we live in it.

4 And I saw thrones, and they sat upon them, and judgment was given to them. And I saw the souls of those who had been

beheaded because of the testimony of Jesus and because of the word of God, and those who had not worshiped the Beast or his image, and had not received the mark upon their forehead and upon their head; and they came to life and reigned with Christ for a thousand years.

Now we see something else going on during the thousand years. Thrones are given for those who died during the Tribulation who would not worship the emperor, but proclaimed the Word of God. Those who face death as Jesus did will rule with Him for the thousand years. During the Tribulation they were counted as criminals because they were Christians. During the Millennium they will rule as Kings and Queens, because they did not deny the faith even unto death.

5 The rest of the dead did not come to life until the thousand years were completed. This is the first resurrection.

This event is called the first resurrection. The second resurrection will come in vv. 12–13. So there is in this chapter the two resurrections and two deaths. If the first readers will be faithful unto death they will taste the first death but they will also be a part of the first resurrection and they will not have a part in the second death.

6 Blessed and holy is the one who has a part in the first resurrection; over these the second death has no power, but they will be priests of God and of Christ and will reign with Him for a thousand years.

The book of revelation has a basic purpose; to convince believers to face death, if need be, in witnessing for Jesus. There is a carrot-and-stick approach. The stick is if you deny Jesus He will deny you, and you will be cast out with the unbelievers. The carrot is if you die witnessing for the faith you will wear white, be with God, and reign with Christ. This one seems to be for this group in this Tribulation. They will rule with Christ but only for a thousand years. Suffering for Jesus is an honor that God rewards. Those who suffer for Jesus the first death because they would not deny His name, and would not be hurt by the second death. They will be a part of the first resurrection and will have to wait with everyone else for the second resurrection.

They are blessed and Holy if they give their lives this way, and will always be remembered by the Church. They will not be thought of as criminals as Rome tried to make them out to be. They will reign with Christ where He is reigning. Their reign is only for the thousand years. Christ will reign forever. There were Jewish expectations as to how long the reign of the Messiah would be. Some speculated many thousands of years; but Christ will reign forever. The Kingdom of God, announced by John the Baptist and Jesus, came in when Jesus rose from the dead; and was open for business at Pentecost. The Kingdom of God has not ceased and Jesus still rules the Kingdom of God. The Kingdom of God has no end.

7 And when the thousand years are completed, Satan will be released from his prison.

This is the last verse to deal with the millennium and more questions are raised than answered. We will look at some of these questions later in the book. For now, let us recap what has been stated. During the thousand years:

1. Satan will be bound and locked up.
2. Satan will not be allowed to deceive
3. Those who stand for Christ even in the face of death will rule with Christ.

These things have happened in history. Following Roman persecution, there was a time when the church was free from the oppressive misinformation and lies of Satan, and they were able to teach the world the Gospel. Those who died for the faith during the Tribulation were called saints (a word that changed in meaning) and were seen as ruling with Christ. That time when the saints ruled is called now by historians the Age of Faith, and Middle Ages.

We now live in that short time in which Satan is let loose to lie and distort the truth again.

8 and will come out to deceive the nations which are in the four corners of the earth, Gog and Magog, to gather them together for the war; the number of them is like the sand of the seashore.

9 And they came up on the broad plain of the earth and surrounded the camp of the saints and the beloved city, and fire came down from Heaven and devoured them.

We need to see this war with the saints in the same way we saw the war between the Beast and the false prophet on one side and Jesus and His church on the other side. This is the final war as recorded in Ezekiel 38 & 39. Is it a literal attack on the Nation of Israel, or symbolic of a worldwide attack on the people of God? Either this shows a military plan of the final attack or it is symbolic of the way the world gangs up on God's people. I believe it is symbolic but it could go either way. Ezekiel is also a symbolic book.

Gog and Magog were ancient nations (Genesis 10:2) and are seen as the enemies of God, or God's people. However the battle takes place, Heaven will answer with fire.

10 And the devil who deceived them was thrown into the lake of fire and brimstone, where the beast and the false

prophet are also; and they will be tormented day and night forever and ever.

Satan's short time comes to a close and he now joins the Beast and false prophet in the Lake of Fire. He does not get out of this one. Evil will finally be defeated. We live in the short time while Satan is raging and lying and spouting his misinformation. It is good to know that it will come to an end. It will only come to an end when Jesus returns.

11 And I saw a great white throne and Him who sat upon it, from whose presence earth and Heaven fled away, and no place was found for them.

After Jesus returns Judgment comes (Matthew 25). Revelation does not tell us of the rapture that Paul talks about in 1 Corinthians 15:51–52, and 1 Thessalonians 4:13–18. So we are left to assume that just before the fire falls the believers are taken out of the world.

In the beginning when God created the Heaven and the Earth, He saw it and said that it was good. Now sin so corrupted creation, heaven and earth cannot stand before the Holy God. Is this the destruction of the earth? Could the fire from Heaven be a nuclear holocaust such as is suggested by Billy Graham's *Approaching Hoofbeats*? 2 Peter 3:10 tells that the world will be consumed with a roar and intense heat. Could it be that Christ takes His church out of the world and the men left to themselves, without Christ or the church, blow themselves up? Or will the fire be a judgment from God?

12 And I saw the dead, the great and the small, standing before the throne, and books were opened; and another book was opened, which is the book of life; and the dead

were judged from the things which were written in the books, according to their deeds.

However the world is destroyed, John sees all the dead. The superstars and regular folk stand before God to find that all their deeds have been recorded. We are judged by our deeds and not our beliefs, because what we do proves what we believe (Matt. 7:24–27; James 1:22). None are saved by their works but those who are saved have works.

Separate from all the other books that record the deeds of men is the Book of Life. We first hear of this book from Moses (Exodus 32:32–33). After Moses talks to God, he tells us about a book which he no doubt learned about on the Mountain of God. David also knows about this book (Psalm 69:28), and so does Paul (Philippians 4:3). Those whose names are written in this book are saved by grace.

13 And the sea gave up the dead which were in it, and death and Hades gave up the dead which were in them; and they were judged, every one of them according to their deeds.

Everyone who ever lived will stand before God. It makes no difference if the dead are buried or laid in a cave tomb, or lost at sea, or burned in a fire. No matter what happens to the body, the same God who made the first body will give you another one if need be, and you will stand before Him and give an account for what you have done in your life.

14 And death and Hades were thrown onto the Lake of Fire. This is the second death, the Lake of Fire.

Now that death and Hades have given up the dead that are in them, there is no reason for them to continue. These evils are thrown into the Lake of Fire.

190

15 And if anyone's name was not found written in the book of life, he was thrown into the Lake of Fire.

Whatever your deeds are, the only salvation comes when your name is written in the Lamb's Book of Life. If your name is not written in that book, you are thrown into the Lake of Fire with Satan, the Beast, the false prophet, and all the others. You may have not done anything as bad as they did; but what you did not do is trust Christ for your salvation. That's how people's names get into the Book of Life. Some of their deeds are just as bad as some of those who are in the Lake of Fire. The only difference is that the one listed in the Book of Life repented of his sins and called on Jesus to save him from his sins. His sins were paid for on the cross of Jesus. The one in the Lake of Fire, decided that he did not need Jesus to save him from his sins.

There is a final exam and the answer to the test has been given out. Do you really feel sorry for anyone who fails the test?

For I consider that the sufferings of this present time are not worthy to be compared with the glory that is to be revealed to us.

—Romans 8:18

"When Christ calls a man," says Dietrich Bonhoeffer, "he bids him come and die."

In February, when the Gestapo prison in Berlin was destroyed by an air raid, Bonhoeffer was taken to the concentration camp of Buchenwald and from there to other places until he was executed by special order of Himmler at the concentration camp at Flossenburg on April 9th 1945, just a few days before it was liberated by the Allies. This happened just about the time when his brother Klaus and his sisters' husbands, Hans von Dohnanyi and Rudiger Schleicher, met their execution at the hands of the Gestapo in Berlin and in the concentration camp at Sachsenhausen.

—April, 1945, The Cost of Discipleship, by Dietrich Bonhoeffer,
Foreword, p. 7; Memoir, p. 21

21

The New

1 And I saw a new Heaven and a new earth; for the first heaven and the first earth passed away, and there is no longer any sea.

Now we see the new Heaven and new earth that Isaiah 65:17–66:24 talks about. Now the lion eats straw with the ox, and the wolf and the lamb shall graze together. Read Isaiah and you will see that those things belong here and not in the millennium.

There is no longer any sea. The sea that separated Heaven and earth, God and man, John and the seven churches, is gone. There is no more separation.

2 And I saw the holy city, new Jerusalem, coming down out of Heaven from God, made ready as a bride adorned for her husband.

John received this revelation in A.D. 90, the Old Jerusalem was destroyed in A.D. 70. The Old Jerusalem is gone; it's the New Jerusalem that is coming. The New Jerusalem will be the home of the people of God, but it is not made by the hands of men as other cities are, but comes down from God. This is the city that Abraham is looking for in Hebrews 11:10.

3 And I heard a loud voice from the throne, saying, "Behold, the Tabernacle of God is among men, and He shall dwell

among them, and they shall be his people, and God Himself shall be among them.

John begins his Gospel by telling us about the Word. In John 1:14 he tells us that the Word became flesh and tabernacled among us. Jesus is our Tabernacle. Jesus is God. When Jesus lives among his people then God is among them. God told Moses to build the Tabernacle so that He may dwell among His people (Exodus 25:8).

The desire of God, to be the God of his people, is a regular Old Testament theme. In Leviticus 26:12 God told Moses of this special relationship that should be between God and His people. But the people sinned so that they left God for other gods that are not gods. In Ezekiel 37:23, 27 God took notice of the sin and said that one day he would bring his people from the nations and again be their God. Paul applied these words to Christians who are now God's people (II Cor. 6:16).

4 and He shall wipe away every tear from their eyes; and there shall no longer be any death; there shall no longer be any mourning, or crying, or pain; the first things have passed away."

When this happens they will not have the problems they have now. They will not be crying for loved ones they have lost to government persecution, or any death. Death and mourning and crying and pain are all part of these first things we still live with. In that day all these things will be gone. I heard R. C. Sproul say that when he was a child and hurt himself, his mother would come and wipe away his tears and that was very tender, but it was temporary. When Jesus wipes away our tears it is not temporary.

194

5 And He who sits on the throne said, "Behold, I am making all things new." And He said, "Write, for these words are faithful and true."

God will make all things new. When we became Christians all things became new for us, for we have become new creatures (II Cor. 5:17). Yet we still live in an old world with the old rules. God will make a new world that fits new people.

6 And He said to me, "It is done. I am the Alpha and the Omega, the beginning and the end. I will give to the one who thirsts from the spring of the water of life without cost.

God is eternal. Those who hunger and thirst for righteousness will be satisfied (Matt 5:6). Isaiah 55:1 is a call for anyone who is thirsty to come and drink freely. Jesus gave the same call on the last day of the Feast of Tabernacles, in John 7:37 (also see John 4:4–14). You can pay as much money as you want for things that don't satisfy or you can receive the living water from Jesus.

7 "He who overcomes shall inherit these things, and I will be his God, and he will be My son."

We are in the world, but we must overcome the world, the flesh, and the devil. We cannot believe Satan's lies and have victory. To the seven churches, overcoming means not worshipping Caesar, only worshipping God through Jesus. Do not deny the Faith even unto death. We must still seek the truth behind through the devil's lies, which the world believes and teaches. We must also not deny the Faith even unto death. God will be our God and we will be His sons and daughters because of what Jesus did for us on the cross.

8 "But for the cowardly and unbelieving and abominable and murderers and immoral persons and sorcerers and idolaters and all liars, their part will be in the lake that burns with fire and brimstone, which is the second death."

Those who are not faithful unto death are cowards. Cowards have their place with all the other unbelievers.

But wait a minute. "What about the security of the believer?" you may ask.

Well, I believe in the security of the believer and I believe in the insecurity of the make-believer. I do not have a list of the Elect and I don't know anyone on earth who does. The only such list is in the Book of Life, but I haven't seen it and no one on earth has seen it. I do believe one way to distinguish the believer from the make-believer is that the believer is faithful unto death. When the going gets tough the make-believers find a way to avoid making a stand for Jesus.

9 And one of the seven angels who had the seven bowls full of the seven last plagues, came and spoke with me, saying, "Come here, I shall show you the bride, the wife of the Lamb."

Now John is invited by one of the angels he has seen earlier (we do recognize individuals in Heaven) to see the bride; but it is not a person, it is the city that God has made.

10 And he carried me away in the Spirit to a great and high mountain, and showed me the holy city, Jerusalem, coming down out of heaven from God,

11 having the glory of God. Her brilliance was like a very costly stone, as a stone of crystal-clear jasper.

The city which has come down from God has the glory of God in it. It shines like costly jewelry. John watches from a high mountain just as Moses did (Deuteronomy 32:48–52) and as Jesus did (Matthew 4:8) to get a good view of this new city.

12 It had a great and high wall, with twelve gates, and at the gates were twelve angels; and the names were written on them, which are those of the twelve tribes of the sons of Israel.

13 There were three gates on the east and three gates on the north and three gates on the south and three gates on the west.

14 And the wall of the city had twelve foundations of stones, and on them were the twelve names of the twelve Apostles of the Lamb.

A great city has a great wall. This wall has twelve gates, and the names of the twelve tribes of Israel are on those gates. Just as the twelve tribes camped around the Tabernacle with three tribes on each side; so the gates surround the city. There are also twelve foundations for the twelve Apostles of the Lamb. Reminders of the Old and New Covenants surround the city.

15 And the one who spoke with me had a gold measuring rod to measure the city, and its gates and its wall.

16 And the city is laid out as a square, and its length is as great as the width; and he measured the city with the rod, fifteen hundred miles; its length and width and height are equal.
17 And he measured its wall, seventy-two yards, according to human measurements, which are also angelic measurements.

It's a big city, laid out like a square. With the measurements we are given if one corner was in Los Angeles, and another corner was in Louisiana, then the other two corners would be in British Columbia and Ontario. If it is just as high as it is wide, then it would be just about the size, but not the shape, of the moon. But we don't get the correct symbolism if we just see for size, for it is not recorded in miles but in stadia. We should translate it not at fifteen hundred miles, but at twelve thousand stadia. A stadia is about 600 feet, so twelve thousand stadia equals fifteen hundred miles. You get an idea of the size but you don't get an idea of the symbolism that is in the number when you use miles. The symbolism is in the number. Twelve is the number of the people of God magnified by a thousand.

The wall is not 72 yards but 144 cubits. $144 = 12 \times 12$; 12 is the number symbolizing the people of God.

> 18 And the material of the wall was jasper; and the city was pure gold, like clear glass.

> 19 The foundation stones of the city wall were adorned with every kind of precious stone. The first foundation stone was jasper; the second, sapphire; the third, chalcedony; the fourth, emerald;

> 20 the fifth, sardonyx; the sixth, sardius; the seventh, chrysolite; the eighth, beryl; the ninth, topaz; the tenth, chrysoprase; the eleventh, jacinth; the twelfth, amethyst.

The twelve costly stones are the same as the stones that were in the breast-piece of the High Priest (Exodus 39:8–15). The gold of the city being clear as glass, and tells us more about first-century glass than it does about the city.

21 And the twelve gates were twelve pearls; each one of the gates was a single pearl. And the street of the city was pure gold, like transparent glass.

I want to see the gates, but I also want to see the clams! The streets, like the city, are of this glassy gold. These things that the world fights for, kills for and covets. Gold lines the streets of the Golden City. Solomon had such a wealthy kingdom that silver was not worth anything because there was so much gold. In this city there is so much gold . . . will the gold be worth anything at all? Worth will not be on a gold standard but on God's standard.

22 And I saw no Temple in it, for the Lord God, the Almighty, and the Lamb, are its Temple.

23 And the city has no need of the sun or moon to shine upon it, for the glory of God has illuminated it, and its lamp is the Lamb.

24 And the nations shall walk by its light, and the kings of the earth shall bring their glory into it.

25 And in the daytime (for there shall be no night there) its gates shall never be closed;

26 and they shall bring the glory and the honor of the nations into it;

There are a few things this city does not have. It has no Temple. It does not need one. As in the Garden of Eden, God just walks through it. It has no need for lamps or sun or moon, for God is the light of the world. There is no night. The gates never close.

The glory of the nations is brought into the city. Unlike the Temple where the Gentiles were kept out, here they are

199

brought in. Whatever is good in the nations will be brought into the city.

27 and nothing unclean and no one who practices abomination and lying, shall ever come into it, but only those whose names are written in the Lamb's Book of Life.

Only those redeemed by the Lamb and who have their names written in His book can enter into the city. Sin is not an issue anymore.

You men who are stiff-necked and uncircumcised in heart and ears are always resisting the Holy Spirit; you are doing just as your fathers did.

Which one of the prophets did your fathers not persecute? And they killed those who had previously announced the coming of the Righteous One, whose betrayers and murderers you have become.

—Acts 7:51–52

The guards, driven by fear or perhaps guilt, came to his cell in the night with long poles and cruelly thrust them between the cell bars to jab the doctor into unconsciousness. Somebody figured wrong. For one night the battle was over, and, though no one heard Bill Wallace cry, "It is finished," he offered up his spirit and brought his ministry and mission to a close. Quietly, his soul slipped from his torn body and his exhausted mind and went to be with the One he had so faithfully and unstintingly served.

Bill Wallace was dead to the world, but was alive forever with God.

—February, 1951, *Bill Wallace of China,* pp. 149–150

22

The Invitation

1 And he showed me a river of the water of life, clear as crystal, coming from the throne of God and of the Lamb,

The land of the Bible is a land like Southern California; that is, basically a desert. Water is necessary to life. Four Rivers came from the Garden of Eden (Genesis 2:10–14). God is the source of life, and his throne is the source of this water. As Psalm 46:4 says, "There is a river whose streams make glad the city of God." Jesus promised (John 4) ". . . Whoever drinks of the water that I shall give him shall become in him a well of water springing up to eternal life." The water is symbolic of the Holy Spirit giving life to us.

2 in the middle of its street. And on either side of the river was the tree of life, bearing twelve kinds of fruit, yielding its fruit every month; and the leaves of the tree were for the healing of the nations.

In the Garden of Eden there was a tree that was not eaten of by Adam and Eve (Genesis 2:9). It was there for them to eat of, but the other tree got all their attention. After the fall, steps were taken to make sure that the Tree of Life would not be accessible to those in a state of sin (Genesis 3:22–24). The tree of life is the cross of Jesus.

This tree does not bring forth one fruit once a year as most trees do, but rather 12 fruits, 12 months of the year. Even the leaves heal the nations.

3 And there shall no longer be any curse; and the throne of God and of the Lamb shall be in it, and His bond-servants shall serve Him;

The curse that came after the fall is not lifted and God and Jesus live in the City. His bond-servants get to do what they to do, serve their God.

4 and they shall see His face, and His name shall be on their foreheads.

We shall know as fully as we are known (I Corinthians 13:12). Jesus promised that the pure in heart will see God (Matthew 5:8). We have seen in Revelation that everyone has a name on his forehead, either of the Beast or of God. As in Ezekiel 9:4 & 6, and in Revelation 7:3, God so marked his people who stayed faithful to Him. His name that no one knows will be on their forehead.

5 And there shall no longer be any night; and they shall not have need of the light of a lamp nor the light of the sun, because the Lord God shall illuminate them; and they shall reign forever and ever.

Night is that time of darkness that hides men's evil deeds. When Judas went to betray Jesus, John tells us that it was night (John 13:30). The repetition of facts reflects the emotion of the celebration of the Victory of God.

6 And he said to me, "These words are faithful and true;" and the Lord, the God of the spirits and the prophets, sent

203

his angel to show his bond-servants the things which must shortly take place.

7 "And behold, I am coming quickly. Blessed is he who heeds the words of the prophecy of this book."

God testifies to the faithfulness of this prophecy and that these things must shortly (from John's own day) must take place; and I believe they did take place.

The last of the seven blessings of Revelation takes place for those who obey the words of the prophecy, don't worship Caesar, and are faithful to Jesus no matter what.

Jesus is coming quickly. After He comes we will say, "That was quick!" So far it has been 2,000 years, and it may be another 2,000, but it will be quick. (See "Things We Cannot Know" in the Introduction).

8 And I, John, am the one who heard and saw these things. And when I heard and saw, I fell down to worship at the feet of the angel who showed these things.

9 And he said to me, "Do not do that; I am a fellow servant of yours and of your brethren the prophets and of those who heed the words of this book; worship God."

Either John makes the same mistake twice (19:10), or more likely he records it twice. It's good to recount the incident because it shows that: 1. Angels should not be worshiped; only God. 2. John is human and can make mistakes also. 3. Angels are fellow servants of God. 4. Again the Book of Revelation must be obeyed.

10 And he said to me, "Do not seal up the words of the prophecy of this book, for the time is near.

Daniel was told to seal up the prophecy for it was not for his time; it was for the future, or end times. The visions Daniel saw did not come to pass for several hundred years. His prophecies would not come to pass for several hundred years. His prophecies would not come to pass until Daniel was long dead and gone. It was not for him or his generation, so he was to seal up the prophecy till the day came when they were to be fulfilled. Revelation is for John's day and he must not seal up the words of this book. The seven churches and all the churches of that day needed to know that they must stand up for Jesus.

11 "Let the one who does wrong, still do wrong; and let the one who is filthy, still be filthy; and let the one who is righteous, still practice righteousness; and let the one who is holy, still keep himself holy."

This, to me, is the scariest verse in the Bible. Daniel is told at the end of this book that the wicked will act wickedly and they will not understand the prophecies (Daniel 12:10). But this is different. This is more like saying, "Go ahead and sin." You do not defeat God by sinning, you only defeat yourself. Nor should we be discouraged by those who reject the Gospel. We must also be careful not to join them but keep ourselves pure. This verse is shocking because we believe it is our job to reach out to everyone and stop them from sinning. Our real job is to tell the good news that people can be free from sin. God does the saving.

12 "Behold, I am coming quickly, and My reward is with Me, to render to every man according to what he has done.

13 "I am the Alpha and the Omega, the first and the last, the beginning and the end."

Jesus is coming back to judge all men. We do things according to what we believe. If we really believe then we are faithful unto death. If we do not believe we will worship Caesar rather than face death. It is our deeds that betray our belief. It is our deeds that He will judge (Matthew 8:21; James 1:22).

14 Blessed are those who wash their robes, that they may have the right to the tree of life, and may enter by the gates into the city.

Our only hope is to wash our robes, our souls, in the blood of Christ. Just as the Children of Israel put the blood of the Passover Lamb on their door posts so that the death angel would pass over their houses, so we who are sinners and deserve death must wash in the blood of Jesus. That means we must become Christians and accept the Grace of God that saves us from our sins. Only then does this book mean good news for us. Only then will our names be written in the Lamb's Book of Life, and we can enter this marvelous City. We understand that this is symbolic language, for the Apostle Paul tells us in I Corinthians 2:9 "Things which eye has not seen and ear has not heard, and which have not entered the heart of man, all that God has prepared for those who love Him."

15 Outside are the dogs and the sorcerers and the immoral persons and the murderers and the idolaters, and everyone who loves and practices lying.

The Bible is not unaware that there are always those who will not turn from sin and trust Jesus. Their deeds tell what they really believe.

16 "I, Jesus, have sent My angel to testify to you these things for the churches. I am the root and the offspring of David, the bright morning star."

Jesus confirms the message of the angel to the churches. He is the root of David; that is, He is the one who created the world and Adam so that Adam could have children, and his children have children, till we come to David, and He is also the offspring of David (see Luke 3:23–38). The Bright and Morning Star lets us know that the long night and darkness is over.

17 And the spirit and the bride say, "Come." And let one who hears say, "Come." And let one who is thirsty come; let the one who wishes to take the water of life without cost.

The Invitation is given here at the end of the Bible. The Holy Spirit invites you to come to Jesus. The Bride, the church herself, invites you to come to Jesus. The Spirit asks the church hearing this letter as it is read aloud to say to you, come. Jesus died for you. He came that you might have life, and that more abundantly. Here again we come back to the invitation Isaiah gave and Jesus gave (Isaiah 55:1–2, John 7:37). If you thirst, that is if life has left you dry and you are looking for something that satisfied, if you have a desire to know God, the Holy Spirit is calling you to trust Jesus. Pray right now and ask Jesus to be Lord of your life.

The Salvation that God offers to all men is free. Men seek satisfaction in life with things that cost money and do not satisfy (Isaiah 55:2). Salvation is free to us because the price has been paid. It is not cheap, it is free. We have been bought by the blood of Jesus (I Peter 1:18–21).

18 I testify to everyone who hears the words of the prophecy of this book; if anyone adds to them, God shall add to him the plagues which are written in this book;

19 And if anyone takes away from the words of the book of this prophecy, God shall take away his part from the tree of life and from the holy city, which are written in this book.

Jesus adds a warning to the Book of Revelation. An apocalypse by its very nature is easy to misunderstand. This book has an important message and it should not be lost. I do not believe that the curse belongs to us who would teach what we think the book means, as long as we are careful to make a distinction between our ideas and the Words of God, as God warned us in Deuteronomy 4:2 (also see Deuteronomy 12:32 & Proverbs 30:5 & 6). We must never teach as the word of God our own doctrines. We must not make up stuff just to be clever.

Revelation is a difficult book at best and needs some explanation. But our explanation must never be confused with the text. And never should we take the confusing parts of this prophecy and announce: the date for the end of the world, give me all your money, I'm the new leader of all truth or any other silly thing. If you purposely mislead using this book I believe this curse belongs to you. The Bible is a Holy book and needs to be treated as such. You must become a Christian if you would see the City, but you must respect the Word of God or you will be on the outside with all the other lairs of v. 15.

20. He who testifies to these things says, "Yes, I am coming quickly." Amen. Come, Lord Jesus.

The testimony comes from Jesus Himself, and He reminds us that He is coming soon. Joseph told his brothers that God would one day take them out of Egypt and when this took place, they were to bury him in the Land of Promise. That promise was made in Genesis (50:25) but it did not take place until the end of Joshua (24:32) 400 years and 5 books later. It would have been easy for anyone to give up hope that Joseph's idea would come about; but it was more than an idea, it was a promise from God. Daniel saw the future from his place in Babylon. He saw future kingdoms come and go, even up to the Messiah coming and establishing His Kingdom. Hundreds of years have gone by and everything happened as Daniel saw it. God keeps his promises. Jesus is coming soon. The church is still eager to have him come.

21. The grace of the Lord Jesus be with all. Amen.

Pastmillennialism: A Study of the Book of Revelation

But as at that time he who was born according to the flesh persecuted him who was born according to the Spirit, so it is now also.

—Galatians 4:29

Sung Du had gone to seminary and prepared for the ministry. After being ordained, he had taken a church near Suyang-Ch'on. Then the Communists came and put him to work as a slave laborer in a mine. Because he refused to work on Sunday, they beat him so badly they thought he was dead. "They carried my brother out and threw him in the river," Sung Ho lamented. When they turned away, some of his church members jumped in and pulled his body out. They took him back to the village and were preparing for his funeral when they found he was still alive. Many months later he was well enough to preach again.

But then the Communists came back and arrested him again. This time they shot him and made sure he was dead. So he died twice.

—Early 1950s Korea, *By Their Blood,* by James & Marti Hefley, p. 98

23

A History of Millennial Thought

Eusebius wrote the first history of the Church 300 years after Luke wrote Acts. Writing about an earlier writer who had a lot of second- or third-hand records of miracles and sayings of Jesus and the apostles, Eusebius says:

> "Papias reproduces other stories communicated to him by word of mouth, together with some otherwise unknown parables and teachings of the Saviour, and other things of a more allegorical character. He says that after the resurrection of the dead there will be a period of a thousand years, when Christ's kingdom will be set up on this earth in material form. I suppose he got these notions by misinterpreting the apostolic accounts and failing to grasp what they said in mystic and symbolic language. For he seems to have been a man of very small intelligence, to judge from his books. But it is partly due to him that the great majority of churchmen after him took the same view, relying on his early date; e.g. Irenaeus and several others, who clearly hold the same opinion." (Eusebius 39:11, p. 152)

Whether or not Papias began the Chiliastic movement, (an early Millennial movement using the Greek word for 1000) by the time the church emerged from persecution there were two different views of the Book of Revelation. The popular Chiliastic view taught a rather materialistic view of the coming Kingdom of God. Eusebius, who came later and had read documents now gone, believed that Revelation was written for the churches going through Tribulation. The Chiliasts got so excited about the glories of the Millennium that they read Jewish writings in order to add to the excitement.

Although the reign of the Messiah was to be the reign of righteousness, it was often conceived of in terms of material blessings. "The earth also shall yield its fruit ten thousand-fold, and on each vine there shall be a thousand branches and each branch shall produce a thousand clusters, and each cluster shall produce a thousand grapes, and each grape a cor (120 gallons) of wine" (2 Baruch 29:5, 6). There will be no more disease, no more untimely death; the beasts will be friendly with men; and women will have no pain in childbirth (2 Baruch 73), (Barclay, v.2 p. 188)

Those who held this view came to be known as Chiliasts because of the Greek word for "1000." (Millennium comes from the Latin for the same number.) All Scripture was interpreted in the light of the two verses (Rev. 20:3, 5) dealing with the thousand years. Every physical as well as spiritual blessing would be there. I believe that just as the Jews made the Messiah so wonderful that they did not recognize him when He came, so Chiliasts made the Millennium so wonderful that no other blessing would ever seem good. They began to look forward to that blessed time instead of the Blessed Hope. They were more concerned with the Chiliasts than with Christ.

The extreme abuses of the Chiliasts caused Augustine to pour cold water on the whole idea of a Millennium (and not for the purposes of baptism). While other details changed, (and the popular preachers of the day never did stop teaching of the glories of the coming thousand years), the official view of the Middle Ages was that the Millennium, like other things in Revelation, was largely symbolic for the church age. Augustine taught that the Church was the Kingdom of God and would continue to replace the influence of the evil world until the coming of Christ; and this church age is the Millennium.

If you lived in the Millennium it would be hard to see it (like seeing the forest for the trees). You also had to hold on to the view that the Lord could return at any time. Augustine believed he lived in the time symbolized by the Millennium, and so do I. The popular view was still Chiliast or futurist. Still others saw the thousand years as just that and begin to feel them come to an end. In A.D. 1147, Gerard of Poehlde wrote to Evermord, prior of a monastery on the German frontier: "Look upon the conditions of the time and you will find it full of dangers. In Revelation, John prophesied that Satan would be freed after a thousand years have passed from the time of Constantine and Silvester when in Heavenly fashion, peace was granted to the Holy Church after the triumphant struggle of the martyrs. Thus, Satan meditating on the long-desired end of this peace now almost completed, shakes the chains binding him." (Zoba, Wendy Murray, Future Tense, *Christianity Today* October 2, 1995, p. 20.) Even after the Millennium was over people taught and still teach that the Millennium is symbolic of the church age and we are still in it. To them Satan is still bound, and apologetics are not needed, just proclamation.

The Reformers had much to do with the rest of the Bible and really had little to do with Revelation. Luther called it a book of straw, and Calvin quite seriously questioned whether it should be in the Canon at all. Yet the Reformers did find it interesting that the enemy of faith should be Rome (which of course was also where their enemy was; only this time it was the Church and not the government). This they could preach. The historical view followed this basic idea by saying that Revelation was the unveiling of the history of the Church from John's day to this. This being of course the time in which the writer was writing. The main problem with this view is that it must always be updated. Yet because it pointed to Rome as the Antichrist, this view came to be held as the Protestant view. As histories needed to be changed because history just refused to stop, more Protestants became Amillennial.

Amillennial, you remember, does not mean no Millennium but that the Millennium has a symbolic meaning, and we are not sure what that meaning is. Others are sure of the meaning and to them it means it is the Church age and we are still in it, and Satan is still bound, as he was in Augustine's day.

In 1830 Margaret MacDonald, with her sister and brother ran their own house church in Scotland. Gifts of the Spirit and "true Christianity" led them away from all others, and they just worshiped in their home, with visions and prophecies.

Margaret prophesied that Jesus would come back secretly, and "rapture" or catch up, select ones of the saved before the Great Tribulation; then Jesus would come back again for the rest of the elect, judge the earth, and set up the Millennial Kingdom. This is the first time a secret rapture was ever taught. Before this, Premillennialists historically taught that Jesus would come back before the Millennium, but only once, to judge the world and set up the Kingdom. The Church would therefore go through the Great Tribulation. Not a pleasant prospect to preach. (Mc-Pherson, Dave. *The Incredible Coverup, The True Story of the Pre-Trib Rapture.* 1975 Logos International) This also means that Jesus comes back twice, once for the church and again for judgment.

Visiting the MacDonald house were many who wished to experience, investigate, or observe the "moving of the Spirit." Two of those were Edward Irving, founder of the Catholic Apostolic Church in England, and John Nelson Darby. Both held independently that the happenings at the McDonald household were not of the Spirit (the McDonalds had the same opinion of the ministries of Irving and Darby) and both began to teach a secret rapture. While Irving had some other teachings that made him easy to dismiss, Darby was a very popular preacher and evangelist. In his preaching he incorporated this secret rapture into a system of a Bible world view known as Dispensationalism, whereby God acts in different ways in different ages.

According to this teaching we would be in the Church Age dispensation, and the next dispensation to come would be that ushered in by the rapture and would be called the Great Tribulation. Darby's theology was made more popular when his Bible notes were added to the King James Bible and published by C. I. Scofield in 1909. The 1900s in America were the height of the Modernist/Fundamentalist debates in which the Scofield Bible became the standard under which Fundamentalist Bible Believers marched.

This new teaching of a secret rapture (which did not exist before 1830) became in the twentieth century a rallying cry for Fundamentalists, and was absorbed into mainstream and/or conservative Protestant Evangelical thought in America. In many churches the secret rapture is one of the fundamentals of the faith. If you don't believe in the secret rapture of the Church, you are a liberal in the minds of many believers. The amazing thing about the teaching is that it was accepted by people claiming to get their theology only from the Bible. This interpretation did not originate from exegesis of the Bible (or someone would have found it sooner). The same preachers and theologians who would condemn Joseph Smith for his visions accepted these visions with no problem.

In America during the late 1800s and early 1900s, our heads were turned with the progress of science, of man and his machines, and the healing of modern medicine. Churchmen began to think that with education, science, and the preaching of the Gospel we would bring in the Millennium through doing good works and making the world a better place. Then Jesus would come back after the Millennium. Those who believed this changed governments, built hospitals, orphanages, homes for unwed mothers, rescue missions, sent out missionaries and changed the world. They made their world better. Thus postmillenial teaching was very popular until war again raised its ugly head. If the world is getting better and better there should be no more wars. World War I was called the war to end all wars and was justified in that way.

World War II became another matter. It became clear that man was still sinful and this world was still in trouble. Pearl Harbor, Dachau, Ravensbruck, Hiroshima and the Cold War that followed all took their toll on the postmillennial view, and most who held this view became Premillennialist or Amillennialist.

Before we criticize this group too much we need to look at what they accomplished. It is easy in our Pre-Mill age to attack the Post-Mill age for the prophecy that did not pan out. Yet, while their beliefs led them to accomplish many things for the Kingdom of God, our Pre-Mill views led us to do nothing until He comes to take us out of here. Escapism led the way among conservative Christians. When anyone would say that the world was getting bad, the reply would be, "Good! That means that Jesus is coming back soon." Then it became evident that all that was necessary for evil to triumph was for good men to do nothing. Jerry Falwell and others began to get premillennial Christians out of their Escapist mode and got them socially active despite their eschatology.

We are to be salt and light. We must speak out against wrong. We must be found doing good works, and provoking one another to good works. Believe whatever view of the Millennium you wish, but do the work of a postmillennialist.

Now I rejoice in my sufferings for your sake, and in my flesh I do my share on behalf of His body (which is the church) in filling up that which is lacking in Christ's afflictions.

—Colossians 1:24

Missionary work in the Long Baliem Valley continued despite the danger. In 1957 Australian Baptists occupied the north end. By 1962 they had won several hundred converts. On September 30 a large force of pagan Danis launched war on about sixty villages and killed scores of Christians. One of the martyrs was heard to tell another as attackers approached, "Pray my brother, pray, the enemy is upon us. If we die we ascend to be with Jesus."

It was customary for defeated villagers to flee to another area. But the survivors announced to the local Australian missionary, "We will stay. We need you and you need us. We will rebuild." And they did.

In 1966 Stan Dale, an Australian member of the Regions Beyond Missionary Union was hit by five arrows while trying unsuccessfully to save two Yali Christians from death. In September 1968, Dale and colleague Phil Masters were ambushed on the bank of the Seng River. Their bodies were found riddled with arrows from warriors of the Yali tribe.

—1960s New Guinea, *By Their Blood,* by James & Marti Hefley, p. 182

24

Millennial Questions

1. And I saw an angel coming down from heaven, having the key of the abyss and a great chain in his hand.
2. And he laid hold of the dragon, the serpent of old, who is the devil and Satan, and bound him for a thousand years
3. and threw him into the abyss, and shut it and sealed it over him, so that he should not deceive the nations any longer, until the thousand years were completed; after these things he must be released for a short time.

These are the only verses on the Millennium that we have. You may (as others have done) apply other verses to these but if you do you would, I believe, be taking them out of their context to apply to something entirely new. I believe that the Millennium was a prophecy for the Seven Churches in Asia Minor who were going through the Great Tribulation (Which tribulation is the Great Tribulation? It's the one you are going through at the moment!)

I think before we get to the questions we need to see what the only verses on the Millennium have to say.

1. Satan is bound for a thousand years.
2. During this time he cannot deceive the nations.
3. Saints who have suffered for Christ will reign with Him for this Thousand Years.
4. There is a first and a second Resurrection.

5. There is an end to this Millennium.

The late Dr. Fred Fisher in his seminary class on Revelation, shared with us his questions and answers about the Millennium and they inspired me to ask some more questions.

Dr. Fisher's Questions

1. When did the binding take place?
2. How did this binding take place?
3. How does it affect Satan's power?
4. How long will it last?
5. What does "loosing" Satan mean?
6. When will this take place?
7. Why will this take place?

This led me to ask some questions of my own. It also helped me to understand how much we really do not know about the Millennium. While the answer to each question depends on your view of the Millennium, some questions cannot be answered. Here I have combined my own question with Dr. Fisher's questions.

1. Is the Millennium literal or spiritual?

2. What does this Millennium look like? Would we know it if we saw it? Is it a time of perfection? Do we know perfection when we see it? Is it a time of wealth, happiness, piety? What will it (or did it) look like?

3. What does it mean to bind Satan? What does this do to his power? When Satan is bound are his demons bound?

What does Satan do? If we isolate that, we can see if there was a time in history when we got along without him.

4. Is the Millennium local or universal?

5. How do the Saints reign with Christ? How does Christ reign?

6. Why does the Millennium end? Why just a thousand years? What is its purpose?

1. Is it literal or spiritual? Was it 1,000 years, or did the thousand years mean something else in Revelation drama? We believe God is Sovereign. We see here a small glimpse of something God did, does, or will do, and good Christian scholars disagree about what it means. There is a strong possibility (because we disagree with each other) that most of us, or all of us, are wrong about what this means. We should not hold our views about the Millennium the same way we hold the clear truths of Scripture. I therefore would suggest a different view. An older, forgotten view. That the Millennium is a literal thousand years.

The argument Summers puts forth in his excellent book, *Worthy is the Lamb,* is flawed when he says that "The chain is not literal; one would hardly use a literal chain on a spiritual being. The thousand-year period is no more literal than the chain." What he should have said is that it is legitimate to interpret the Book of Revelation in a symbolic way. The question is not whether the chains were literal about whether they were physical, i.e., iron or gold. Physical chains could be understood to be a symbol for something else. However, if an angel brought the chains, and angels are spirit beings also, then he would bring the kind of chains that would do the job. That Satan is a spiritual being does not

222

mean that he cannot be bound, nor does it prove that the whole context must be understood in a symbolic way. God, for a thousand years, limited or stopped completely Satan's activities. The thousand years could be a symbol of something, but I do not believe it is. I believe that it is a literal thousand years in history. I believe there was a literal thousand years in which Satan was bound. Most Christians in America believe that the Millennium is yet future and that Christ will come to earth to reign in a physical way on the earth. They then take many of the verses of the Old and New Testaments that properly belong to the New Heaven and the New Earth and apply them to the Millennium. This confuses the whole issue. The thousand years during which Satan is bound is much different from the time that Jesus rules the earth from Jerusalem, and the ox and lion, lamb and wolf all eat grass. Clearing this up will help us go on to what the Millennium is all about.

2. What did the Millennium look like? It looked like the early Middle Ages. What historians would call the Age of Faith.

Would we know it if we saw it? No, because we are always looking for something else. Satan knows how to get us looking in the wrong direction so that when something good comes we want something else. When Jesus came, the Pharisees and even his own disciples were expecting Him to fulfill their idea of what the Messiah is supposed to be. Before he was to be bound, I believe, Satan left a poisoned apple for the church to chew on while he was bound: a thousand years of happiness, health, wealth, and all your dreams coming true. (Not even Heaven is a place where all your dreams come true, it's a place you cannot even dream of unless all you dream of is Jesus and His Glory), because Heaven is about Him, not you and me. If you want a place where all your dreams come true, read *Voyage of the Dawn Treader,* by C. S. Lewis. The Chiliastic movement was so worldly in its outlook it led Augustine to search for a better alternative to the thousand years. Augustine was the first Amillennialist.

Was it a time of perfection? No. To bind Satan still leaves us with the world and the flesh. We can sin quite well without him. James tells us where our sin comes from in James 1:14–15:

> But each one is tempted when he is carried away and enticed by his own lust . . . Then when lust has conceived, it gives birth to sin; and when sin is accomplished, it brings forth death.

Later we will see what Satan does; for now it is enough to recognize that not everything in that time was good, nor should we strive to be like the believers of that time.

Do we know perfection when we see it? I don't think so. The Pharisees did not recognize perfection. When it walked up to them they hit Him in the face. I don't think we are any better than they were. We need to hunger and thirst for righteousness in order to see it. Was there wealth, happiness, piety? Yes, as in all ages of man, there were those who were wealthy and those who were happy, but they were not always the same ones. There was also piety and depravity. What did it look like? It looked like the early Middle Ages. When "the basic purpose of life was salvation of the soul, not the search for scientific fact or the control of nature or other goals which have preoccupied the lives of people in other eras. Whether or not he lived fully on this earth was of secondary concern to a medieval man so long as he achieved salvation in the next life." (*Civilization Past and Present;* T. Walter Wallbank, p. 222).

3. What does it mean to bind Satan? What does this do to his power? When Satan is bound are his demons bound? What is it that Satan does anyway? Jesus told us that he lies and murders (John 8:44). His lies kill and he prompts others to kill. He cannot sin for us, as we saw earlier in James 1:14–15, but he tempts us; and until we are covered with the Blood of Jesus we are powerless before him. He blinds the minds of unbelievers (2 Cor. 4:3–4). He slanders, attacks, accuses, tempts and stalks the Saints. The Saints of the Tribulation are victorious over Satan and for a thousand years the whole world will know that.

For a thousand years Satan will be bound, but not totally defeated. Is he totally out of the picture? He's bound; is he gagged? Are his demons bound, or on their own? These questions remained unanswered, but some things are clear. While Satan is bound he cannot deceive the nations. His lies stop. The Church can preach the gospel without the constant vicious attack and distortion of a super-intelligent adversary. During this time Satan is gone but the flesh, the world, and sin are still very much alive. Total depravity is still in man. Man is free to follow God, but does he want to? We always point to limitations that keep us from greatness, but what if they disappeared; would we press on to greatness or just lose another excuse?

4. Is it local or universal? It is assumed that the Millennium would be a world-wide rule, and it probably could have been, but it was not. Remember, the Book of Revelation was written to the seven Churches of Asia Minor. Those seven Churches, after the time of tribulation, lived in a Christian Empire that lasted for 1,000 years. Their land did not see war. It was a time that those John wrote to could not imagine.

If Satan is bound from deceiving the world then that blessing would be universal, yet many of the blessings we think of were local to the Eastern or Byzantine Empire. (See *A History of the Millennium.*) At the same time the East and Constantinopole enjoyed blessings, Rome and the West received the plagues of the book.

5. How do the Saints reign with Christ? How does Christ reign? However Christ reigns is how the Saints reign. In the time that John wrote, Caesar ruled the world and the saints were so criminal that they were put to death by the government. The Government determined what was right. Rome made the laws based on what Rome thought was right. Then God determined what was right and condemned that government. The world then knew that the Roman Government was wrong and Christ and the Saints that Rome put to death were right. Right and wrong are now determined by what Christ and the Saints said. Therefore Christ and the Saints rule. When Laws were made and Church Councils formed, the words of Christ and the Saints were consulted and the words of the Caesars were forgotten. Everyone knew that Christ and the Saints were right about the Gospel and Rome was wrong. This is the vindication the Saints asked for in Rev. 6:10.

6. Why does it end? Why just a thousand years? The hardest question about the Millennium is "why does it end." It is a bigger question for those who see a perfect future Millennium. If it is so perfect, why stop? What is the purpose of the Millennium? Christianity can't make its case to the world if Satan is always twisting her words. A break from the Great Liar gives us the chance to make our case to the world, and gives Christ's church a break from all the tribulation.

For you, brethren, became imitators of the churches of God in Christ Jesus that are in Judea, for you also endured the same sufferings at the hands of your own countrymen, even as they did from the Jews,

who both killed the Lord Jesus and the prophets and drove us out. They are not pleasing to God, but hostile to all men

hindering us from speaking to the Gentiles that they might be saved; with the result that they always fill up the measure of their sins. But wrath has come upon them to the utmost.

—1 Thessalonians 2:14–16

Christmas 1990 had barely passed when Father Lazar's flat was broken into and he was murdered with "a heavy metallic object." He had been entrusted by Metropolitan Iuvenalii with an investigation—there was said to be a corruption surrounding the late Patriarch Pimen that involved the KGB. All his electronic aids as well as his briefcase disappeared.

In March 1991, a third murder occurred. This time Father Serphim, a thirty-three-year-old priest-monk, was assassinated, mutilated while he was still alive.

—1990s Russia, *Their Blood Cries Out*, by Paul Marshall, p. 124

227

25

Objections to the Millennium

The Middle Ages? Are you nuts? In this day and age we are trying to live down the Middle or Dark Ages! It is always brought up to us as a day of faith and not reason. It is said that if they left the world to us Christians we would take the world back to the Dark Ages.

G. K. Chesterton had a great answer to this when he said: "I take in order the next instance offered: the idea that Christianity belongs to the Dark Ages. Here I did not satisfy myself with reading modern generalizations; I read a little history. And in history I found that Christianity, so far from belonging to the Dark Ages, was the one path across the Dark Ages that was not dark. It was the shining bridge connecting two shining civilizations. If anyone says that the faith arose in ignorance and savagery, the answer is simple: it didn't. It arose in the Mediterranean civilization in the full summer of the Roman Empire. The world was swarming with skeptics, and pantheism was as plain as the sun, when Constantine nailed the cross to the mast. It is perfectly true that afterwards the ship sank; but it is far more extraordinary that the ship came up again: repainted and glittering, with the cross still at the top. This is the amazing thing the religion did: it turned a sunken ship into a submarine. The ark lived under the load of waters; after being buried under the debris of dynasties and clans, we arose and remembered Rome. If our faith had been a mere fad of the fading empire, fad would have followed fad in the twilight, and if the civilization ever re-emerged (and many such have never re-emerged) it would have been under some new barbaric flag. But the Christian Church was the last life of the old society and was also the first life of the new. She took the people who were forgetting how to make an arch and she taught them to invent the Gothic arch. In a word, the most absurd thing that could be said of the Church is the thing we have all heard said of it. How can we say that the Church wishes to bring us back into the Dark Ages? The Church was the only thing that ever brought us out of them." (p. 154, Orthodoxy, 1908).

As great as this defense is it is missing a couple of things. First the term "Dark Ages" was coined by folks in the Enlightenment. They looked back and said they were better than their fathers (1 Kings 19:1–4). According to this theory, mankind was improving right along from Egyptian to Greek, to Roman, and then Christianity came along and bam! We were all in darkness. Now that we have enlightened the world we can get on with life. This is what Chesterton was addressing. But it was only a dark time because it did not have their light. And what was their light? Science. The task of the person in the Middle Ages was not to find the scientific answer to every problem. The task of the person in the Middle Ages was to be sure he missed Hell and made Heaven. What good does it do us today to live with every scientific wonder and still be lost, without Christ, and Hell bound. Science cannot keep us from Hell or bring us to God. It is not in the realm of science to do such things. All science can do is claim there is no God, or Hell, or Heaven for that matter. Science cannot prove this, it can only claim it (Psalm 14); a foolish thing to do .

From the beginning, science or knowledge was always a gift with a bite to it. From the time that our parents partook from the Tree of Knowledge it was of good and evil. The Evil One told them and us that this is the way to find, or more to the point, to be like gods, to have this new knowledge. The knowledge itself is not evil but it has good and evil applications. Every labor-saving device and modern invention has a military application. In the Middle Ages they had all the knowledge they wanted, but knew that the real knowledge they needed was how to save their souls. In the Middle Ages they could call on the wisdom of the Greeks who had figured most things out (such as *Ptolemy's Almagest*) to tell them the size and shape of the earth, the relation to the sun and such as that. But what will get me saved?

The wisest ancient was not Greek, but Hebrew. He tried everything man can live for, money, power, women, wisdom, foolishness. He had it all and was in a unique position to tell us what is the best. We find the answer in the Book of Ecclesiastes: none of those things satisfy. All you can do is fear God and keep His commandments. This applies to everyone, because God will judge. (My poor paraphrase of Ecclesiastes 12:13–14) The wisest man that ever lived agreed with the folks in the Middle Ages. Seeking God is the priority in life.

Further, far from bringing civilization into darkness Christianity always encouraged wisdom from whatever source. Biblical religion led men *from* superstitions, not *to* them. Protestant Christianity taught us that the search for truth could lead good men to disagree. All of the great early scientists were Christian. But the unique feature of Christianity—to oppose slavery—brought about the Industrial Revolution. The Greeks had designs for steam engines yet they did not build them because there was no necessity; slaves could always do the work. Slaves could always be the answer to the question until the churches taught that slavery was wrong. (Islam has not yet taught that, for today in the Sudan slaves are still sold.)

The Dark Ages theory has another problem with the facts, and that is that in the West the problem was not that they had been overcome with darkness, but that they were overrun by hordes of European savages who had to be converted and educated, basically built from the ground up. The Western churches went from a situation where educated Romans were in charge of the government to a new group of savages coming from the north who were now in charge, and wanted to be Roman and Christian.

The Western churches were busy for a long time because just as soon as they would get one group half-way trained (the process takes generations) another group would come down. But if we read history this way we have a great gap in our story. There is what I call an "undiscovered country" for most of us, because in history we kept going West. The part that was not in darkness was the East.

Dr. Philip Sherrard sates it this way:

In this scheme of things, there is a strange kind of gap or hiatus between the decline of the Roman Empire and the rise of Renaissance Italy. The civilized world is supposed to have suffered an eclipse. Not even the glories of Charlemagne's court and the brilliance of medieval scholarship are of any consequence. It is assumed that from A.D. 400 to A.D. 1400 the progress of the arts and sciences, and indeed all cultural life, came to a halt.

This version of history is more than an oversimplification: For between the old Roman Empire and the Renaissance lay the great age of Byzantium. It endured for some eleven centuries, and formed a strategic bridge between antiquity and the modern world. It not only preserved the two unifying elements of the Roman Empire—Roman law and state organization, and the inherited tradition of Hellenic

231

culture—it added a third and even more powerful force: Christianity." Sherrard, *Great Ages of Man, A History of the World's Cultures: Byzantium.* Time-Life Books, 1996, p. 12.

Dr. Sherrard goes on to say the question is not why civilization went blank for a thousand years, but why the history of the Byzantine Empire is so unknown. I think of three reasons. One is that we like to move west in history, especially those of us in America. Moving east from Rome back to Constantinople is the wrong direction. The second reason is race; we want to see ourselves in history. As soon as we get to Rome (a Western city), we don't follow civilization back East, we stay West with our fathers, even though they were savages. Some even begin to speak of England. If you want to follow civilizations you must do what they say you should do in understanding politics: "Follow the money." In every age there has been a nation or people who were blessed by God, to lead the world. With the power and culture has been a great amount of wealth. Daniel only talks about 4 or 5 of these empires. Before Babylon there was Assyria, Egypt, and Israel under David and Solomon. Many nations have had their day in the sun. In the Middle Ages it was Byzantium that had the culture, money, and power. But we would rather talk about our great, great, etc. grandfathers who were savages, or just converted savages. If you really want to think well of yourself, don't read too deeply into the history of Europe; wait till after they had been civilized. (No, I don't know when that is; better to ask Frances Shaffer.)

The third reason that the Byzantine world has been ignored is the last point of Dr. Sherrard; you cannot speak of that world without discussing Christianity. In America today that is anathema. Religion in America at the end of the twentieth century does not exist, as far as the classroom is concerned. Constantinople is not the only gap we have in history. We don't understand the Puritans (why were they so glum?), or the Founding Fathers they influenced. We don't understand Prohibition or the Revivalism that brought it. We wouldn't even know why there are churches at all if all we had were American history classes. But if you are an honest historian you cannot ignore the Age of Faith. For a thousand years men put belief at the top of their agenda, no matter what their circumstances. Whether you talk about West or East it is an age of faith, so why would people turn away from the Eastern Empire?

The West had a lot of things going on. It was not a united Christian nation for a thousand years. It was, in the beginning, barbaric. The priests in the West were not very powerful until after they had converted barbaric leaders. Then it was a long time till they truly converted the common people. Then another barbaric tribe would come south, or West. By the time the Church came to full power in the West, the Millennium was over, and corruption was in the Church. The Church in the East had its problems, also, but there is no question that the Church was the most important influence in the Eastern Empire.

Am I trying to say that this was a perfect time and we should be like them, Roman Catholic, or Eastern Orthodox?

Not at all. Again, it was a time when Satan was bound, but the world and the flesh were alive and well. What I am trying to say is that this was a time when God gave the churches and all Christians and even the world a great gift, a world without Satan. He did not give them all knowledge, but He did get rid of the liar. He did not get rid of the war spirit in the heart of man, but He did get rid of the one who encourages such a spirit to war at all times. It was still up to the people who lived in the Millennium to follow the truth.

The opportunity to rule with Christ during the Millennium came to those to whom John wrote. If you are faithful unto death you will rule with Christ from His Throne. (Revelation 3:21; 20:4–6)

Therefore, we ourselves speak proudly of you among the churches of God for your perseverance and faith in the midst of all your persecutions and afflictions which you endure.

—2 Thessalonians 1:4

Bishop Fan Xueyan, perhaps the most influential of China's underground Catholic bishops, died in police custody on April 13, 1992, the day before his ten-year sentence would have expired.

Color photographs taken on April 16 or 17 showed large marks on his forehead and on one cheek. Both legs appeared to be dislocated below the knee. No definitive analysis as to the cause of death could be made from the photos, but the marks were consistent with violence suffered shortly before death.

—1992, China, *Their Blood Cries Out,* by Paul Marshall, p. 79

26

Looking for and Dating the Millennium

When we look at history to see if something fitting the Millennium took place, first of all we have to understand what we are looking for. We are not looking for the Lion to lie down with the lamb or ox, without rising in a short while to eat his friends; that comes when God brings in the New Heaven and a New Earth (see Revelation 21:1 and Isaiah 61:10). Nor are we looking for a time when people live in sinless perfection and everything they do is wonderful. While Satan is bound there is still the world and the flesh, there is still sin.

The world has no great ideas of its own and is by nature a follower. It does not want to be surrendered to the will of God and so it will look for any reason, any loophole it can use to make the best of things while its favorite ally is locked up. What Satan does for the world is give it lies: reasons not to believe or trust God, His word or His Church. When Satan is not around, the Church must refute the lies and present reasons for faith. Was there a time when the Great Deceiver was not twisting the words of Scripture, or passing out his lies? The World still resisted the truth but had no reason to disbelieve.

The flesh is weak when the spirit is willing. The flesh can be counted on at all times to let us down. If Satan was bound, our own tendency to sin, our own total depravity, would still be there. With Satan not there to snatch away from the truth (Matthew 13:19) we could hear the Gospel and find the Grace to be saved, but we would still need the salvation, justification, and sanctification, because we are still sinners; even without Satan.

We are not looking for subtle fulfillments such as the working of a king or priest on a certain day, but of an age, a thousand years. We are looking for attitudes, beliefs and world views to change, and then after a thousand years change again. Satan's absence would make a difference.

We are looking for a time, not a perfect time, just a time, when the lies stopped. The whole truth may not have been known but The Liar was not telling his lies and the truth of the Gospel had a chance. The Church had a great opportunity, whether it took full advantage of that opportunity or not. Do we ever take full advantage of the opportunities God gives us?

There was a time that the world did not follow everything God said but believed that: God created the world, Jesus is the Son of God who died to redeem mankind, that there will be a coming judgment of God, that there is a Hell to miss and a Heaven to gain, and that the most important thing a man could do is get right with God so that he would go to Heaven and not Hell. They also believed that the saints were right to die rather than to deny the Faith; that the government of Rome was wrong to execute the saints who stood for the faith and were recalled with Christ as someone to remember, as someone who was still alive and as someone to model one's life after.

So what are we looking for? A time when Satan is bound. Now that's somewhat difficult. How do you find a time when something is not there? Even when that thing is there it is invisible; you can only see the effects. It's a time when the nations are not deceived.

It's also a time when the saints who underwent persecution come to reign with Christ. Now this is called the First Resurrection. Others did not come to life, only those who were persecuted for the Faith. Everyone will come to life in the General or Second Resurrection.

Now it does not say where this will take place. Is it on earth or in Heaven? Well, we have a clue in Revelation 3:21; Jesus says to the church at Laodicea, "He who overcomes, I will grant to him to sit down with Me on My throne, as I also overcame and sat down with My Father on His throne." When Jesus sat down at the right hand of the Father it was not on earth but in Heaven, and that was reflected in the hearts and minds of the believers. When the Tribulation saints witnessed to their Lord by giving themselves over to the enemy in death, it was a witness to the world and to other believers. It was also a proof that Jesus is raised from the dead and has conquered death, for his followers had no fear of death.

The tribulation, or persecuted, saints did rule on earth with Christ in the hearts of the world. All believers of the time called on the saints as quickly as on Christ. You may like it or not but that's what they did.

Is there something in history that looks like the Millennium? Yes, the Byzantine Empire. Here at the same time is wealth, education, even gas lamps on the streets (streets that did not see war for a thousand years), and trade and work for the people. Education, art, science, (such as it was), philosophy, and theology were all inside these walls. I've found the Millennium! From the Galerius Edict in 311 when Christianity became legal, to 1453 when Constantinople fell to the Turks was more than a thousand years. So like Gerard of Poehlde, (see page 317) I dated the Millennium from Constantine and Silvester (Bishop of Rome at the time; roughly between 330 and 1330. Then I began to search the history books looking for a time without the influence of the Evil One. I found that it is easier to find when he reappears than when he is bound.

On further reflection I thought of inertia. Things in motion tend to remain in motion. If Satan were suddenly, overnight removed from earth for a thousand years, people would not wake up the next morning and say, "Hey now, I think I will quit doing evil and be a Christian." Things do not work that way. People would still carry on traditions they were used to until they found a good reason not to. It would take the Church time to demolish the walls and gates set up before Satan left. The reverse is also true. When Satan comes back, the Church has the inertia. He has to work hard at destroying foundations that the Church set up. Historians tell us that the latter persecutions of the Church by Rome were carried out but without the usual zeal. The first years of the Millennium would still be a time of tribulation, at least officially. It would be up to the Church to get the world to stop the persecution.

Paganism made its official last stand in Julian the Apostate (although it was not the end of paganism); all the other kings of the Roman Empire East and West were Christian. Historian Norman F. Cantor says:

> Julian's rule, however ineffectual, nevertheless encouraged the Roman aristocracy to resist stubbornly the advance of Christianity and left the problem of the survival of paganism in the western half of the empire even more difficult than it had been before Julian's apostasy. The emperors in the sixth and seventh decades of the century, although Christian, refused to help the church suppress paganism and adopted a policy of religious impartiality and tolerance. It was only in the eighth decade of the century that the church again succeeded in obtaining the support of the Emperor in suppressing the remnant of Paganism. (1963, *The Civilization of the Middle Ages* Norman F. Cantor, HarperCollins)

It took the Western Church almost the entire thousand years to stamp out the lies of paganism. The edict of Milan did not wipe out paganism, it just reflected the changing times. Those who used logic to make their decisions could not but choose Christianity over paganism. Those involved in superstition, tradition, sexual perversion, and emotions to make their decisions held out longer. The battle for the minds of men was won in large measure because the enemy could not supply men of logic with any other answer. The world does not need the truth to reject Christ, just a good excuse. They don't need *the* answer, just *any* answer; anything to give them the excuses they need for disobedience to God.

At the other end of the Millennium the Church has the traditions that are hard for Satan to break. Now I am thinking A.D. 100–1100. If Revelation was written in A.D. 90 and there was $3^1/_2$ years Tribulation, that would place it about A.D. 94 for the binding of Satan to take place, and A.D. 1094 for him to be loosed. But that is more specific than I want to be.

For me the Millennium was not a time when things were great but an opportunity for things to be great. However you draw the line, there was a thousand years when man's minds were fixed on God.

It is a trustworthy statement:
For if we died with Him, we shall also live with Him;
If we endure, we shall also reign with Him;
If we deny Him, He also will deny us;
If we are faithless, He remains faithful; for He cannot
deny Himself.

—2 Timothy 2:11–13

On June 24, 1994, Mehdi Dibaj was on his way
to his daughter's birthday party in suburban Tehran.
He disappeared.

On July 5, the body of Mehdi Dibaj was found in
a Tehran park.

During his ten-year imprisonment, Dibaj wrote to
his son, "I have always envied those Christians who all
through the church history were martyred for Christ
Jesus our Lord. What a privilege to live for our Lord
and to die for Him as well."

—1994, Iran, *Their Blood Cries Out,* by Paul Marshall, p. 24

27

History of the Millennium

I'm not a historian, I don't even play one on television. I do not have time here to write, nor do you have time to read a thousand years of history of the Eastern and Western churches. If you do, I recommend a few histories in the bibliography. I do want to give you a few impressions I have found in reading about the time.

To understand the Millennium, you must go back to the days of persecution. Lies that Satan told and the world believed were that: Many gods created the world and cause much turmoil. Nothing you do in life matters; history runs in circles; one god is as good as another and you can play one against the other, but you can't trust any of them; they will all get you.

As the Church came on the scene, Satan told more lies: that the early church were a bunch of atheists because their place of worship did not have an idol; no idol, no god. The world also believed that Christians were immoral because as a part of their service they would have a meal and they would exclude non-believers, and you can just imagine what goes on behind closed doors! The world also believed that the Church was cannibalistic because when you listened at the closed door you would hear some one say "eat my body," and "drink my blood." The Church was also bad for business. Idol makers, prostitutes, and slave traders, could see where this type of thinking would go. Also, bad times were blamed on the church because she led people away from the old gods. The old gods are the older lies.

The lies lead to action by the State to put an end to this illegal cult. There were crucifixions, arrests, torture, public beatings, seizing property of individuals and Church buildings, burning at the stake, human beings left to be eaten in the arenas by wild animals, or slain by gladiators. These tactics usually worked for Rome to change public opinion and stop movements. It did not work for the Church; it could not be broken or stopped. As a matter of fact, it seemed that those efforts helped the Church to grow. I believe when Satan was bound that the persecution did not stop. The historians tell us that while they were carried out it was not with the same vigor as before; a vigor inspired, perhaps, from below.

Inertia, or tradition, or pigheadedness, or a lack of a better idea, keeps people going through their routine. While the transition was going on the Church could see some progress. Under normal circumstances when the Church would answer the world's questions (called apologetics) the world would come up with another question, and pay no attention to the first answer. But now they were listening, and even those who did not believe began to sympathize. Well into the Middle Ages apologetics was not needed. The old lies had been answered and there was no one to create new lies. The first half of the *City of God,* by St. Augustine, was written against the old gods of Greece and Rome.

Emperors varied in their hatred for the Church (or the appeasing of the pagan lobbies) or non-hate, until one came to the throne and made Christianity legal. ''In 311 the Emperor Galerius saw the failure of the efforts at suppression, and issued an Edict of Toleration, making Christianity a legal religion in the East. Later the emperor Constantine was swayed toward Christianity . . . In 313 he issued the Edict of

Milan, which legalized Christianity throughout the Empire and put it on a par with the pagan cults . . . By 395, the end of the reign of Emperor Theodosius, Christianity was the sole and official religion of the State." (1967, *Civilization Past and Present*, by T. Walter Wallbank, Alastair M. Taylor, and Niles M. Bailkey, published by Scott, Foresman, and Company).

Now we can see the problems created by being so closely associated with the state, but the church then went from hiding to ruling with the government. While we see the problems, if we had the opportunity to do the same thing some brothers would rush right to Washington—some already have.

Another change came about in that the Empire was divided into two. It's really a tale of two cities. Old Rome in the city of Rome itself, and new Rome created by Constantine—and named for himself, Constantinople. The original idea was to have two capitols, one for the East and one for the West. However, the Western city was dying.

The story of the Millennium is a tale of two cities. Both of theme embraced Christianity but they did not always embrace each other. Old Rome in the West was the real Rome, but it was no longer the capital city it once was. She was yet to receive all the plagues due her because she had persecuted the Church. The East, however, was the home of the seven Churches that John wrote to. The Eastern capitol that Constantine ruled was the capitol of Christianity, and it would continue to be so for over a thousand years. One reason to move the capitol to Constantinople was that the old Senators in old Rome were still steeped in paganism. The new religion would not be challenged in the new capitol.

Because it lasted for a thousand years and was in every sense of the word a Christian Empire (it was the first Christian nation before there were nations), the Byzantine Empire is exciting to my view of Revelation. So I found a history of the Empire, and read it hoping to find a real Christian community in action. The history was mostly about the throne, the most powerful in the world at the time. And it is the soap opera you would expect when power is involved. The only thing Christian about the Emperors is that they went to church, built churches, and from time to time an Emperor would get so caught up in Bible study that he would leave the throne for a monastery. That's different. Like everyone who becomes a Christian, the Eastern Empire did not totally discover all the ways living for Jesus could change their lives. They accepted Christianity but looked to old Roman traditions for their mode of living; nor did they consider changing their form of government. They just baptized what they were doing, like we do. Moving the Empire to the East got rid of the old Senate and left the Emperor to be a total dictator. The Eastern Church called the Emperor the "Vicar of Christ." (In the West the same term is used for the Bishop of Rome, or Pope, which means he is Christ's representative on earth in His absence. Since Jesus promised to be with us till the end of the earth I don't think of Him as absent.)

The Eastern Empire did not deserve to lead the world by their actions during the Millennium any more than the United States of America deserves to lead the world today. The leadership of the world does not depend on your goodness but on the grace of God. God gave his blessings to this great Empire and it's important to notice what they did with it. They built the greatest walls in history. The Great Wall in China did not keep anyone out, any more than the Maginot Line in France did, nor any wall made by man; yet the walls around Constantinople kept everyone out. They took their blessings from God and spent them on themselves and strong defenses.

When the Empire was at its greatest height, Justian I built a church to (as he said) be greater than the Temple Solomon built. The church is Hagada Sophia (Holy Wisdom) and still stands today, although the Turks have turned it into a mosque and now it is a museum; yet it still stands. But having one of the greatest buildings was not enough; they had to get the greatest preacher. The greatest preacher of the day was John of Antioch, and he did not want to come. He did not send in his résumé, as others had when there was an opening. But that was no matter; Constantinople must have the best; so John was kidnapped and brought into the city. His preaching earned him the name Chrysostom (Golden Mouth). And could he preach!

He preached against materialism, sex, sin, oppression of the poor—all the things the upper class of the city loved. While the masses loved John, the upper classes had to work harder to get rid of the great preacher than they did to get him. The powers that be finally won out and God's great spokesman left.

Beware of what you ask for!

In the Middle Ages, East or West, one thing was clear and that was that Christianity and the Bible were true. God worked miracles in the Bible and could do so anytime. They lived in the area where people had died for the faith. They knew the Gospel was true. God created the world. Man was created perfect but chose sin. After the Fall man had a sin nature. Sin is a cancer in the soul that can only be healed by what Jesus did on the cross. The Church is the body of Christ and has authority over my soul. The priest is just a man and may fail, but he speaks for God. Heaven and Hell are real places and it is the most important thing to miss Hell and make Heaven. To do that I must obey the Bible and the Church. The philosophy of the Ancients was brought forward as proof for Christianity. Christianity was seen as true in the same way everything else is true. Truth is not true because it is new; truth is true because it is true. There was no division between Faith and Reason, because the Faith was reasonable. Philosophy was seen as the hand-maid of theology. Theology was the greatest of sciences.

Old Rome had gone to war with the Church and perse-cuted the saints. Old Rome was the harlot that the Emperor Beast rode upon. God prophesied destruction for the city but two things softened and delayed the blows. First Rome quit persecuting the saints and joined the church; and sec-ond—and more importantly—the church prayed for Rome as Jesus taught them to (pray for your enemies—Matthew 5:44). Also, Christians were blamed for Rome's problems because the old gods were being neglected, so Christians interceded for the city. Augustine wrote *The City of God* to address this very problem. Yet judgment still came; natural disasters, moral decline, and foreign invasion fulfilled the wrath of God upon the city that declared war on God's church.

The story in the West was invasion. Before the fall of Rome, one Germanic tribe after another wanted to be in the Empire, not realizing the Empire was no more. Eastern peoples and Northern peoples all came to sack the great city of Rome, not knowing that the city was already sacked to death. The only light left on in the city was that of the Bishop of Rome. Rome, once known as the seat of a great empire, has forever more been known as the home of the church the city sought to destroy.

It became the task of the Western Church to evangelize the different groups coming into the Empire. Education fell with the Roman government which used pay for the people to learn to read. With the government gone, only the church knew how to read, write, and keep records. It was hard enough to make Christians of the European savages; to educate them would take longer. Gregory I of Rome was the first Pope to send missionaries to Northern Europe to win those who had not attacked them yet.

New Rome, Constantinople, ruled near to and over the land of the seven churches. To this land came all the blessings of the Millennium. There was work, money, art, education, culture, and a centralized government to give stability. High walls, a good army and navy and Greek Fire kept the marauders of the West and East out of the Eastern Empire. So while the West struggled daily to keep up with all the newcomers, the East kept them out. The Eastern Church had a higher standard of living, but the West evangelized more. While it is true that the Eastern Church influenced the Russian Church, it's because the Russians came looking for them, not the other way around.

The Eastern Church did not see evangelism or missions as a top priority; their Christianity was more reflective and specialized. One reason is because they always saw dangers beyond their borders, but the real reason is because Christianity began to be understood as limited to the Empire.

To be a citizen of the Empire was to be a Christian. To expand the Empire was to make more people Christian. There was Christianity outside of the Empire, but it was of a very bad quality, to their way of thinking.

The Western Church began to think the same way about its holdings. Missions were not built in the East because they liked to live in luxury behind their walls. The city was security. Yet the world outside did not know Jesus, and as time drew on Christianity became such a part of the state it would be hard for anyone in the city to go outside of the Empire and explain Christianity without the government.

While it was not true or even supposed to be true, Christianity became thought of as two empires. The Kingdom of

God became captured in the East by a race of people and was seen by some to be a race. One man of a different race felt sorry for his people because they still worshiped idols. A wealthy business man, he had people read to him from the Old and New Testaments. He thought: the Jews have their religion and the Christians (seen not as a faith but as a race of people) have theirs, but there is not a good religion for my people, the Arabs.

Muhammad took Allah the moon god, the most popular of all the Arab gods, and Mecca's black rock, and proclaimed a new monotheistic religion. In 622 Muhammad established his religious government in Medina. Ten years later he led his followers to take Mecca. Islam spread with the Koran and the sword. Now most any other time the Eastern Empire or the Persian Empire would have put down this new militant religion, but both had spent all their money and energy fighting each other and there was nothing left for the real problem that would seek to take both over. In 634 the Jihads began. In the Providence of God, this religion became a judgment from God and was allowed to challenge Eastern and Western Christianity in more ways than one. The important question for Christians in the Eastern Empire was "how are you different than them?" In the same way we have to ask ourselves "how are different from the Jehovah's Witnesses or Mormons who come to our door?"

But it was not just theological; much land was taken. North Africa, Palestine and Syria, as well as the Persians, fell to Islam. To the former holdings of the Eastern Empire it was not such a bad thing; the taxes imposed by Constantinople were too high and the people were ready for a change. Moslem persecution of Christians was not as bad in the beginning as it became later. In early Islam Christians and Jews were respected as people of the Book.

Therefore do not be ashamed of the testimony of
our Lord, or of me His prisoner; but join with me in
suffering for the Gospel according to the power of God,
—2 Timothy 1:8

The tiny Iranian evangelical community was sad-
dened but not surprised. The news spread quickly,
house to house, Christian to Christian. "Bishop" Haik
Hovespian-Mehr, the leader of the Assemblies of God,
had been brutally killed.

Bishop Haik had led an international campaign to
save the life of Medhi Dibaj (another beloved Iranian
pastor) who had been imprisoned for a decade on
charges of apostasy, and had been sentenced to death.
On January 16, 1994, Mehdi Dibaj was unexpectedly
released. He walked from prison into the welcoming
embrace of Tehran's rejoicing Christians.

Unfortunately, the long-awaited celebration was
short-lived. Three days after Dibaj's release, Bishop
Haik dropped out of sight. A few more days and his
murder was announced by authorities. His family was
never permitted to see his remains, but a photo of his
corpse was identified by his son.
—1994, Iran, *Their Blood Cries Out,* by Paul Marshall, pp. 23–24

28

A Short History of a Short Time

Islam raised more than theological questions; it also threatened to take over both Eastern and Western Europe. Islam took over Persia, Palestine, Egypt, all of North Africa and then came up into Spain. They threatened mostly the East. This led the East to do something they hated to do: ask their Christian brothers for help. Thus began the time of the Crusades. Pressure would be put on the East. They would ask the West for help; if they got no response they would offer to open talks to reunite the churches. The West would come and the pressure would be removed. Then the events would start all over again.

I've made it sound like all the Crusades were the same, and they were not. Some were total disasters, others were more like diplomatic missions where common sense actually took place. There was a lot of cruelty; but remember that they lived in cruel times, and there were a lot of misunderstandings and outright lies and deceptions. Motives were not always pure. The Evil One was free again and he tempts men to war for all the great reasons.

The first Crusade revealed where the hearts of men were, for they did not fight for a nation or a race; they fought for their faith. Faith was the most important value.

War is just one of Satan's tricks, however. Another of his innovations was the nation-state. This did not exist before the late Middle Ages. It was a new identity for people and a way to see something bigger than themselves that they could be a part of, that was not the Church or Christianity. Before this, if you asked a person who he was, he would say that he was a Christian. After the appearance of the nation-state he would tell you he was an Englishman or a Frenchman, etc. Now men had something else they could kill and die for.

Theology was ingrained into the minds of the people in 1100. Not only did they hold basic Christianity to be true; anyone with education could not deny its truth. Thomas Aquinas even claimed that truth revealed in the Bible could be proven without the Bible. Moving the argument outside of the Bible made it is easier for Satan to win this argument. Years later men could claim that they could prove there is no God, because the proof was outside of Scripture. Aquinas introduced into the West an idea that Islamic philosophers had come up with that reason and Revelation could be separate. What is true in religion is not necessarily true in reason. An idea Islam needed but Christianity did not.

Satan also needed a new place for truth to be found. Truth used to be found in the Church and in God's Word. Satan would need a new place that even the Church would eventually look to for truth. There arose the University. Here Satan could get a foothold because in Greek schools (and Western Education is Greek) everything is questioned; all of your beliefs and truths you held yesterday are questioned again today. It took centuries for Satan to work his way in the arguing of the universities, because Christians kept coming and proving the truth. We will have to come back to the university, but we will see it became a source of truth, not a seeker of Truth.

While Satan waits for theology to percolate he corrupts the religion in the lives of believers. With legalism on one side and super-spirituality on the other, it's easy to make some people either a Pharisee, or a prophet. He whispers

"Grace can be earned," and "Maybe there is an alternative to Hell, why sweat being perfect?" Work's righteousness always works. Now to corrupt the morals of those preachers, money and women and power ought to do it. These things did not always work but they did work with a lot of people. Brave souls fought against these temptations, cowards did not. These temptations were always with men, but now someone was, and is, pushing them and us, a little harder. That the Roman church became corrupt is not the surprise; the surprise is that it took so long. It took so long because good men fought back.

The Crusades bring up a good idea, from Satan's view; as long as we are killing folks in the name of religion, why don't we kill them for getting theology wrong? The theology of most churches leaves salvation by grace through faith alone as Augustine taught it and some well meaning folk have tried to return to the simple Gospel in a corrupt Church. After a couple of failed attempts by John Wycliff and Jan Hus, Martin Luther and John Calvin finally got their point across, yet in the process they broke the unity and authority the church had for so many years.

Now the Universities could kick around Reformation theology; but there was more to talk about. Bacon and Descartes began talking of science in a more important way. Now while the church has never been afraid of any truth, what began to happen is that this science thing became over the years "the truth by which we judge all other truths." Reason began to replace Revelation as the ultimate authority. For example, art doesn't always have to be about religion. "We can paint and sculpt the naked bodies like the Greeks did. The church is so up tight about that because they are narrow and superstitious." Even in the Renaissance they began to call the Middle Ages the Dark Ages because they were beginning to challenge the Church's restraints.

But it was the Enlightenment that really pushed the importance of science. We should have learned from the Garden of Eden that knowledge is both good and evil. With every scientific advance, and I believe they are wonderful, there is a military application. The Enlightened folk began to talk about all truth being scientific truth except faith, which is out of the realm of science. In other words, now there are two kinds of truth, real truth which can be proven scientifically, and faith truth which cannot be proven but only believed. If it is in the Bible it's that faith kind of knowledge and never as good. So if you ever defend your faith against evolution or any other godless myth man has come up with you are dismissed because you speak from faith and they speak from science (despite the fact that Evolution has no scientific proof).

David Hume defined miracles out of existence. Voltaire waged open warfare on Christianity and professed belief in a rational god of deism.

Then some Germans got the idea to study the Bible by scientific methods. They would take secular histories and if they could not find a city or people or place in a secular history, then the Bible must be wrong because history, being a science, is right and the Bible, being a book of faith, is secondary. Theologians bought into the two types of knowledge and began to teach that the Bible was wrong. (Although today we have found through archaeology all those people, places and cities they could not find a hundred years ago.) Things got worse with Higher Criticism. Moses did not write the five books of Moses, Isaiah did not write Isaiah, nobody wrote anything. Theology has been reduced to working an imaginary jigsaw puzzle. By World War II at Cambridge University, C. S. Lewis came under attack for defending Christianity, they would say you are an English professor, leave all the religion to the theologians. His answer was to this effect. I would be glad to but they won't do the job so I must. Lewis could point out the logic where the theologians were wrong but in a university setting only theologians can comment on theology, and they have made a mess of it. You can almost say the bigger the name the university has, the more likely it is that God cannot be found anywhere near their school of theology.

In addition to the teaching of Hume, Voltaire and others who followed them, Friedrich Nietzsche decided that God was dead and that people did not have to obey Him any more. Darwin told us that God did not create the world or us. Sigmund Freud and his followers told us that we don't have a sin problem, just a phobia from childhood.

Satan has used many good men and brilliant people to sell his lies in order to discredit the Bible. But look how long it took for his lies to become the dogma of education. Truth, even scientific evidence is on our side. We can prove our case in a rational way. But, thanks to the Existentialists, rational truth does not matter; what matters is how we feel about things, not what we can prove.

To believe the truth the Bible taught as folk did in the early Middle Ages is today considered backward and superstitious, by the modern educated pagan. In the Church we still believe God's truth and the truth in his Word. What has encouraged me is that from the Millennium on for every crazy idea there has been and continue to be a Jonathan Edwards, C. H. Spurgeon, G. K. Chesterton, C. S. Lewis, Walter Martin, or Josh McDowell and many others who look to the evidence and defend the faith, with a voice like a prophet of God.

The battles still continue although the war was won on the cross. Are you in the battle? We can defeat the giants in our land and destroy "speculations and every lofty thing raised up against the knowledge of God, and we are taking every thought captive to the obedience of Christ." (2 Corinthians 10:5).

The criticism could easily be made that this is an oversimplification of a history of the past thousand years and I agree that is exactly what it is. Others have done better at recording how we have fallen and how the battle is going (I would commend to you Carl F. H. Henry's fine work *God, Revelation and Authority*). My point is simply to bring the reader from the Millennium to the present. As I see the battle, I notice it is not all downhill. We have made strides forward and backward and always we bring the pagans who live around us with us. Marvin Olasky, in *Fighting For Liberty and Virtue,* for instance, points out at a time when England was losing her morals the colonies in America were following the Word of God. Later in the Victorian era England made somewhat of a recovery. The battle goes back and forth depending on whether the People of God take seriously the Word of God.

For to you it has been granted for Christ's sake,
not only to believe in Him but also to suffer for His sake,
—Philippians 1:29

Recent government concern has centered on ex-
tremist Sikhs who want independence for the state of
Punjab. Terrorist attacks by Sikhs and responses by government soldiers have resulted in hundreds of deaths.

Radical Hindus have made a number of attacks on
native Christians. A pastor, known as Brother Abraham,
was bicycling home in Tamil Hadu when he was ambushed. A woman eyewitness working in a nearby field
told police that Brother Abraham was calling, "Jesus,
Jesus, Jesus," as he was chased into a field. There members of a radical Hindu sect caught him and beheaded
him with a sword.

After four of the accused murderers were jailed,
local Indian Christians heard that Hindu extremists
had attempted to bribe police officials to get the
charges reduced. Brother Abraham's wife was asked by
police to sign papers that could exonerate the men who
attacked her husband. She refused.

—India, *By Their Blood,* by James & Marti Hefley, p. 152

29

Eschatology—So What's Next?

So what can we say? Is the world getting better, as the Post-millenialist says, or worse, as the Premillenialist says? Or does it depend on us? I have come to believe that it depends on us. If God's people will live the Gospel, if God's people will believe that God's word is true, and obey it, even with the war raging all around us, and the lies being broadcast on every hand; we can win the battle before us. One day at a time, one battle at a time. The world wants to see the Gospel demonstrated in the life of someone they know.

Now, I know that God has a plan for the end times and He will work out that plan. Whether the last battle in Ezekiel 37 and 38 referred to in Revelation 20:7–9 that end the short time to live in is a real battle, like some say; or if it is a symbolic way of describing the spiritual warfare going on today, I do not know. And I do not care. My job is not to see it all come together; my job is to be obedient in the battle Jesus has put me in right now.

Christians may face a global persecution, as Christians face persecution in Moslem and Communists countries now. I know that there are people in American politics who think getting rid of Christians is not a bad idea. Or we may face many small persecutions between now and then. One thing from Scripture is sure: "In the world you will have tribulation." Jesus tells us in John 16:33 that this world is never going to be at peace with us, but "I have overcome the world."

Corrie Ten Boom and her family might have thought they were fighting the Antichrist as they hid Jews from Hitler's Europe. It was not the last battle, but they fought it well. I cannot help but think if German theologians forty years before had held to the truth, all that evil the world went through would not have happened. Germany was a Christian nation. How could such an Antichrist as Hitler come to power if the shepherds, the pastors, and the Watchmen, (Theologians?) had dealt with the lies Satan threw at them. Hitler would not have been taken seriously, if Nietzsche had not been taken seriously. Nietzsche would not have a foothold if Voltaire had not paved the way. Voltaire would not have been in vogue, if those responsible for truth had held to it. Satan's lies are deadly.

We may see many such battles before the end. Jesus said that till the end life will go on as usual just as it did before Noah's flood (Matthew 24:37–39).This implies that "signs of the times" will not be that clear, it will come upon us suddenly.

Paul tells us in 1 Corinthians 15:50–54 that when Jesus comes back, the dead in Christ will rise first. Then we who are alive will meet him in the air. In New Testament times when the Bridegroom comes to get His bride, He comes from out of the town or village, and the wedding party waits till He comes. When He arrives the wedding party goes out of the town to march in with Him in one big procession. When we meet Him in the air we will be changed to have a body, just like he has, a Resurrection body.

Jesus will judge this world and create a new one. Those who have not received the grace of God to have their sins forgiven, those who have rejected the free gift of eternal salvation will find themselves in Hell. Everyone at the Judgment will watch all the opportunities for salvation they turned away from, and no one will be able to say, "That's not fair!'' God has been more than fair. He has done everything including buy our salvation for us.

These are the plans of God that He has revealed in His word. He has told us again and again that we do not and cannot know the time Jesus will return. The last battle may come, but unless we are in it we are not responsible for it. We are responsible for the next battle. For all we know the next battle is the last battle, or it is hundreds or thousands of battles down the road. We need to be alert and deal with the battle before us now. We do need to quit our star-gazing and pick up the sword and shield and fight to the death the good fight that the saints before us have fought.

We know that we may not win every battle but that some battles can be won. We know that truth can prevail when God's people stand for and believe what God said. We can win the battle. But even if we do win a battle, we have already won the war. And we know our mandate is to be faithful unto death.

who by faith . . .

. . . others were tortured, not accepting their release, in order that they might obtain a better resurrection;

and others experienced mockings and scourgings, yes, also chains and imprisonment.

They were stoned, they were sawn in two, they were tempted, they were put to death with the sword; they went about in sheepskins, in goatskins, being destitute, afflicted, ill–treated

(men of whom the world was not worthy), wandering in deserts and mountains and caves and holes in the ground.

And all these, having gained approval through their faith, did not receive what was promised,

because God had provided something better for us so that apart from us they should not be made perfect.

—Hebrews 11:33–40

Afterword

My purpose in writing is not to lead a new movement, or start an argument, but rather to get into the discussion. The questions Revelation and the Thousand years raise are not answered by Scripture and we will be discussing this till Jesus comes back. When He does come back, and we see how He did it, we will say, "Well, of course that's what it means." Until then we have these questions. If I have convinced you of my view I apologize, for you will have an up-hill battle with other brothers and sisters who believe something different. If I have not convinced you, I hope I made you think about God's Word, and that you continue to study. I have included in the bibliography books from others that helped me, and I believe will help you.

My purpose also was to write a readable book that is theological enough not to embarrass my teachers, but not too technical, so that all who have ears may hear and know what this wonderful book of Revelation means.

I wanted to open this book by saying that for years Revelation was a closed book to me, and I found a way to make it come alive. Yet many books I studied about Revelation began that way so I will end that way. I hope I have helped and not confused anyone. Whatever view you take of this great book, never quit reading, praying, serving, and always be faithful unto death.

Bibliography

Commentaries on Revelation

Alford, Henry *The Greek Testament: ect. V. 4.* Boston: Lee and Shepard, Publishers. 1880.

Ashcraft, Morris. Revelation, (*The Broadman Bible Commentary V. 12*), Edited by Clifton J. Allen. Nashville: Broadman Press, 1972.

Barclay, William. *The Revelation of John Volumes 1 & 2,* (The Daily Study Bible Series) Philadelphia: The Westminster Press, 1976. (Now Broadman Press).

Beasley–Murray, G. R. *The Book of Revelation, (The New Century Bible Commentary),* Edited by Matthew Black. Grand Rapids: Wm. B. Eerdmans Publ. Co., 1983.

DeHaan, M. R. *REVELATION 35 Simple Studies on the Major Themes in Revelation.* Grand Rapids: 1969.

Hobbs, Herschel H. *The Cosmic Drama: An Exposition of the Book of Revelation.* Waco: Word Books, 1975.

Johnson, Alan F. Revelation, (*The Expositor's Bible Commentary V. 12*). Edited by Frank E. Gaebelein. Grand Rapids: Regency Reference Library, Zondervan Publishing House, 1981.

Ladd, George Eldon. *A Commentary on the Revelation of John.* Grand Rapids: William B. Eerdmans Publishing Company, 1972.

Lenski, Richard C. H. *The Interpretations of St. John's Revelation.* Minneapolis: Augsburg Publishing House, 1943.

Newport, John P. *The Lion and the Lamb*. Nashville: Broadman Press, 1986.

MacArthur, Jack. *Expositional Commentary on Revelation*. Eugene: Certain Sound Publishing House, Vernon L. Iverson Co. 1973.

McDowell, Edward A. *The Meaning and Message of the Book of Revelation*. Nashville: Broadman Press, 1951.

McGee, J. Vernon. *Thru the Bible with J. Vernon McGee V. 5*. Pasadena: Thru The Bible Radio, 1983.

Morgan, G. Campbell. *A First Century Message to Twentieth Century Christians,* New York: Fleming H. Revell Company, 1902 (August).

Morris, Canon Leon. *The Revelation of St. John an Introduction and Commentary,* (Tynsdale New Testament Commentaries) Edited by R.V.G. Tasker. Leicester: Inter-Varsity Press, 1983.

Mounce, Robert H. *The Book of Revelation, (The New International Commentary on the New Testament)* Edited by F. F. Bruce. Grand Rapids: William B. Eerdmans Publishing Company, 1977.

Robbins, Ray Frank. *The Revelation of Jesus Christ,* Nashville: Broadman Press, 1975.

Robertson, Archibald Thomas. *Word Pictures In The New Testament V. 6*. Nashville: Broadman Press, 1933.

Summers, Ray, Dr. *Worthy is the Lamb*. Nashville: Broadman Press, 1951.

Sweet, Henry Barclay. *Commentary on Revelation*. Grand Rapids: Kregel Publications, 1977.

Walvoord, John F. *The Revelation of Jesus Christ*. Chicago: Moody Press, 1966.

Wilson, Geoffrey B. *Revelation*. Welwyn, Herts: Evangelical Press, 1985.

Histories and Other Helpful Books

Beasley-Murray, G. R. *Jesus and the Kingdom of God.* Grand Rapids: Wiliam B. Eerdmans, 1986.

Blevins, James L. *Revelation as Drama.* Nashville: Broadman Press, 1984.

Bonhoeffer, Dietrich *The Cost of Discipleship,* Translated by Chr. Kaiser Verlag München. New York: Macmillan, 1961.

Cantor, Nrman F. *The Civilization of the Middle Ages: A Completely Revised and Expanded Edition of Medieval History, the Life and Death of a Civilization.* New York: HarperCollins, 1993.

Chesterton, G. K. *Orthodoxy.* San Francisco: Ignatius Press, 1995.

Clouse, Robert G. *The Meaning of the Millennium: Four Views.* w/George Eldon Ladd, Herman A. Hoyt, Loraine Boettner, Anthony A. Hoekema. Downers Grove: InterVarsity Press, 1977.

Durant, Will. *The Story of Civilization Part III Caesar and Christ: A History of Roman Civilization and of Christianity from their beginnings to* A.D. *325.* New York: Simon and Schuster, 1944.

Durant, Will. *The Story of Civilization Part IV The Age of Faith: A History of Medieval Civilization-Christian, Islamic, and Judaic—from Constantine to Dante:* A.D. *325–1300* New York: Simon and Schuster, 1950.

Eusebius. *The History of the Church from Christ to Constantine,* Translated by G. A. Williamson. Minneapolis: Augsburg, 1975.

Fletcher, Jesse C. *Bill Wallace of China.* Nashville: Broadman Press, 1963.

Foxe, John. *Foxe's Book of Martyrs,* Edited by Marie Gentert King. Old Tappen: Fleming H. Revell Company, 1976.

Fremantle, Anne. *Great Ages of Man A History of the World's Cultures: Age of Faith.* New York: Time-Life Books, 1965.

Gibbon, Edward. *The Decline and Fall of the Roman Empire,* 3 Volumes. New York: Random House.

Graham, Billy. *Approaching Hoofbeats: The Four Horsemen of the Apocalypse.* Waco: Word Books, 1983.

Graham, Billy. *Till Armageddon: A Perspective on Suffering.* Waco: Word Books, 1983.

Hadas, Moses. *Great Ages of Man A History of the World's Cultures: Imperial Rome.* New York: Time-Life Books, 1965.

Haskin, Dorothy C. *In Spite of Dungeon: Suffering for Christ in the Orient.* Grand Rapids: Zondervan Publishing House, 1962.

Hefley, James & Marti. *By Their Blood: Christian Martyrs of the Twentieth Century,* Second Edition. Grand Rapids: Baker Books, 1997.

Henry, Carl F. H. *God, Revelation and Authority: Volume I God who Speaks and Shows Preliminary Considerations.* Waco: Word Books, 1976.

Johnson, Paul *A History of Christianity.* New York: Simon & Schuster, 1995.

Latourette, Kenneth Scott. *A History of Christianity Volume I Beginnings to 1500.* New York: Harper & Row, 1975.

Lewis, C. S. *God In The Dock: Essays on Theology and Ethics,* edited by Walter Hooper. Grand Rapids: William B. Eerdmans Publishing Company, 1970.

Marshall, Paul. *Their Blood Cries Out: The Untold Story of Persecution Against Christians in the Modern World,* with Lela Gilbert. Dallas: Word Publishing, 1997.

McPherson, Dave. *The Incredible Coverup, The True Story of the Pre-Trib Rapture.* Plainfield: Logos International, 1975.

Meyer, Carl S. *The Church: From Pentecost to the Present.* Chicago: Moody Press, 1973.

Norwich, John Julius. *Byzantium: The Early Centuries; Byzantium: The Apogee; Byzantium: The Decline and Fall.* New York: Alfred A. Knopf, 1996.

Olasky, Marvin *Fighting For Liberty and Virtue: Political and Cultural Wars in Eighteenth-Century America* Wheaton, Illinois: Crossway Books, 1995.

Ostrogorsky, George. *History of the Byzantine State,* Translated by Joan Hussey. New Brunswick: Rutgers University Press, 1969.

Qualben, Lars P. *A History of the Christian Church.* New York: Thomas Nelson and Sons, 1968.

Shea, Nina. *In the Lion's Den: A Shocking Account of Persecution and Martyrdom of Christians Today & How We Should Respond.* Nashville: Broadman & Holman Publishers, 1997.

Shelton, Don O. *Heroes of the Cross in America.* New York: The Young People's Missionary Movement, 1904.

Simons, Gerald. *Great Ages of Man A History of the World's Cultures: Barbarian Europe.* New York, 1968.

Sproul, R. C. *The Last Days According to Jesus,* Grand Rapids, Michigan: Baker Books, 1998.

ten Boom, Corrie. *The Hiding Place,* w/John and Elizabeth Sherrill. Washington Depot: Chosen Books, 1971.

Walker, Williston *A History of the Christian Church.* New York: Charles Scribner's Sons, 1970.

Wallbank, Walter T. *Civilization Past and Present* single Volume Third Edition, w/Alastair M. Taylor and Nels M. Bailkey. Glenview: 1967.

Wells, H. G. *The Outline of History: Being a Plain History of Life and Mankind Volumes 1 & 2.* Revised and updated by Raymond Postgate. Garden City: Garden City Books, 1961.

Zoba, Wendy Murray *Future Tense.* Christianity Today, Volume 39, Number 11, October 2, 1995, pp. 18–23.